You Got
DADDY ISSUES ?

By

Polly Walshin

You Got

Daddy Issues ?

By

Polly Walshin

DEDICATION

This book is dedicated to all people who felt they weren't enough based on a lie they believed about themselves. You are and always were plenty! You were always enough, my friend, whether your Dad didn't love you, left you, wasn't there for you, abused you, or neglected you. It had nothing to do with you.

I want to thank everyone on my journey, which became the wind beneath my wings. First, my amazing mother. What can I say about you? You are the reason why I am the woman I am today. I don't know what I would do without you. You are my rock.

Next, my two beautiful kids, you have saved my life and given me a reason to get up every day.

To my grandparents in Heaven, thank you for teaching my mom about Jesus so she could impart her wisdom to me about a genuine relationship and what family truly means.

To my amazing sisters, thank you for loving me and walking me through every single storm.

To my first Pastor, Dr. Sutherland in Memphis from the First Baptist on Get-well, and Mr. Jimmy Lattimer of the Redeemer Church in Memphis, thank you for always loving me as a child and building that rock foundation!

Thank you too, Val, for teaching me deliverance, and to Pastor Jerry for being by me when I was in the desert as a single mom.

Thank you to Meri Crouley for always being the voice straight from Heaven and to Ben Lim for prophesying over my new marriage and giving me hope no matter what.

A special big thank you to Mary and Gary Decker, my spiritual parents, who, every single time I thought I wasn't enough, gave me scripture and told me I was!

To my previous Pastor now, Jim, at Firewheel, you taught me that I still have a destiny and to get off the roller coaster so I can go forth!

To all my best friends, you know who you are from Atlanta to San Diego. You've been there for everything. Thank you for always picking up the phone.

Thank you to my soul mate, my sweet husband. Thank you for finding and loving me! I wouldn't have been able to write this book without your support and cheering me on. I love you.

To my prayer warriors. What would I do without you warring in the spirit for me? Thank you.

I have always had someone to stand beside me and with me through every storm! I am most thankful to my Father in Heaven. He always had my back, even when I didn't have it myself.

TABLE OF CONTENTS

ACKNOWLEDGEMENTS

Today in 2023 and in this post-modern world, we need more father and mother figures to help heal the broken and confused hearts of these young and even elderly people.

I have seen that some of the most immature, toxic, and unhealthy types of people are actual adults and grown-ups rather than young children and adolescents. America needs a comeback of fathers. And in a day and age where transgenderism, sexual confusion, and gender orientation is prevalent, we need good and Godly male fathers to arise and love the Hell out of this generation.

This is not about the patriarchy or being masculine in a dominant, toxic way. This is following the Biblical order of God's blessings and being aligned in the family unit of how the Lord had prioritized the way it should be.

The fathers are the head of the family, and without the presence of good and moral father figures in the community, we will fall prey and victim to a barbaric world of confused and broken people trying to find a name for themselves.

"You Got Daddy Issues," written by my good friend Polly Walshin, is a gut-wrenching, heart-twisting true story that will not only keep you on the edge of your seats as you read this but it will engulf you in the pain and utter rollercoaster ride of being fatherless and left with daddy issues. We all have issues and things that we are dealing with on a daily basis. But how we face them and solve them is many times dependent on the choices that we make, despite how we were taught or raised.

You may have daddy issues of your own. Heck, you may have mommy issues as well! But no matter what the issues are, whether they are veiled and hidden or outright in your face and active, these issues can be dealt with in the loving hands and arms of our Heavenly Father.

"For though you have countless guides in Christ, you do not have many fathers. For I became your father in Christ Jesus through the gospel." (1 Cor. 4:15)

Author Polly Walshin has so openly and transparently shared her story and has opened up her life with grave details and exhilarating scenarios that will seem like an unreal movie. But this, my friends, is the type of thing that happens when there is a systemic problem of fatherlessness in our world. We can end the cycle of "father poverty" today. We can end the cycle of fatherlessness today if we choose to stand up and love in the love of God.

"Greater love has no one than this, that someone lay down his life for his friends." (John 15:13) Will you be a laid-down lover for Jesus or will you allow your issues to lay you down? Do not go another day holding a grudge, a chip on your shoulder, a hint of unforgiveness, or even a scent of magic. Forgive in the name of Jesus and be free inside and out. As you open up and read this book, "You Got Daddy Issues," written and narrated by Polly Walshin, get ready to dive into a very real story of ups and downs, highs and lows, and how the perfect love of God crashes into a prison of fear, abuse, drugs, and violence.

If God can do it for Polly, then God can surely do it for you. I pray that all of your "Daddy Issues" will now become "Daddy's Love Stories."

God bless you.

Th.D., Dr., Pastor Ben Lim
Senior Pastor of Open Heavens World
www.benlimglobal.com

Daddy Issues is an incredible story of overcoming challenges and not giving up! I have known Polly for several years and watched her journey of faith, forgiveness, and forging through the fires and trials of life to the other side - REDEMPTION!

Her story will help others 9nwho have struggled through this journey called Life and believe "that all things are possible" if we TRUST HIM and not GIVE UP! This is a fantastic read, and I encourage you to read this with your heart open and share this with others.

Dr. Meri Crouley

My name in the book is Esther, my daughter asked me what name I would like to choose. My reason is that GOD used her in an extraordinary way to save a nation, and I always saw her as an Old Testament hero in the Bible.

During my daughter's writing of this book, she would send me chapters each time she finished one to have me verify the details were also my memory. Until she wrote this and poured out her heart, I had no idea of the depth of her pain living without a father since she was 10 months old. We all have a heavenly father who loves us and is always there for us if we just call on him.

I dedicate this to all those who have lived without a parent to guide them, that the words in this book will help you and you will come to know your heavenly father who will be your friend in the deepest valleys of your walk thru life and on your highest hills of joy.!"

Love you ,
Momma

INTRODUCTION

FOR ALL THE PEOPLE THAT FELT

THEY WEREN'T ENOUGH!

This book is dedicated to all people who felt they weren't enough based on a lie they told themselves. You are and always were plenty!

This is a deep uncovering of the pain we inflict on ourselves based on not feeling loved or accepted by our parents. In my case, my Dad wasn't there, and I felt rejected.

You have a choice, my friend, to be your POSSIBILITY or your story. This book will help you unlock the pain you have felt and launch you into the future you were always supposed to have.

If you picked this book up, I want you to know this is not a book about sex, nor a book about being kinky or anything like that!! Yes, this book references God, but it is designed for everyone. I picked this cover because she is a dear friend who never knew her own Dad. This caused many struggles in her identity, so I knew it was perfect for this book.

This is a book made for people who never really felt their Dad loved them or never experienced the love from a Dad. This is a book dedicated to the survivors of a narcissistic parent. I will acknowledge my amazing Mom so many times, I hope she gets my love for her.

This is also for all of you single mothers who had to do it all on your own you are heroes. I want to acknowledge all single parents that have picked up the slack left by the absent parent. To the single Moms that sat at home on a Saturday night alone with the baby while their friends went out.

To you single Dads that just sucked it up when your buddies were out, and you stayed home to help your kid with homework or whatever they needed. Fathers like that stuck it out with their wives to be the kind of Dads they were supposed to be. They were constantly there for their kids. You are our heroes.

This is the generation when the famous Bible verses will be fulfilled. Malachi 4:6 says that God will turn the hearts of the Fathers to their children and the hearts of the children to their Fathers.

That's why the timing is just right. It is so fitting that I am finally writing this after wanting to for over 20 years. I am sitting here in my little rental in Point Loma, a mile away from my Mom and my son, and I am finally married.

I have the time during a Pandemic quarantine to write this. I procrastinated for so long in life until finally, God said, "It's time now. I'm going to take away everything that's going to make you not do this." So here I am, finally doing this.

2010 started a decade called the fulfillment of your destiny for a vision for your future. 2020 is the year of clear vision, where all obstacles are removed, and your path becomes crystal clear. God is setting the stage for an exciting new course for all of us!

He is beginning to speak to change so we can, as a culture, move into our true calling and real joy. A divine reset! That change is now here, and I pray that this book encourages you and helps you know that you were **ALWAYS** enough. I believe the enemy or Satan is trying to discourage so many of us in this time because he is the Father of Lies and uses every opportunity to convince us, we are not good enough, not smart enough, not strong enough, not pretty enough, and that we will never really do anything or fulfill our true purpose on earth. Right now, I want you to know that it is a lie straight from the pit of hell. The key here is to fight in faith, fight with the correct thinking, and know that **you are meant for greatness!!!**

Basically, this book is for survivors. The ones that, through all the pain being left by your parents or whomever in your life, managed not to give up! Wherever you are in your journey, I want this book to empower you to know that you are worth it and matter. Please read this book and do whatever it is in your life that will help you for future generations so that you will have the life you were designed to live. I honor you, and I pray my story will help you to see the path we choose usually comes from the pain we've had that we haven't adequately dealt with. Let's create a life based on nothing but the present moment.

These are some common lies children believe. You should take some internal inventory to see if these strike a chord within you.

1. It's your fault your parents divorced.
2. If you were perfect, you could have kept your family together.
3. No one loves you.
4. You were unlovable.
5. You were and are a mistake.
6. Sex is dirty and nasty, but you liked it, so you are dirty and nasty.
7. You are worthless, and you are here sucking someone else's air that deserves it.
8. You attracted this molestation, so you deserved it
9. All men want is one thing which is sex, so you don't believe and receive your husband's love.
10. Sure, God loves the whole world except you; your sins are too big.
11. If anyone got to know the real me, they would reject me, so I keep them at a distance.

12. People only want me for money or what I can give them or do for them.
13. Men only want me for my beauty, not real intimacy, because I'm not worth more than to be a showpiece.

If any of these ring true in your soul, I want you to know they're a lie, and through this book, you will find healing. You will laugh, cry, and identify with so many different things at different levels.

I often wonder why I didn't write this book when I was younger. I know God protected me from myself; I might even be dead. That's the kind of crazy life I've had. I would've gotten caught up in Hollywood and probably would not even be able to write this book.

One of my precious friends said it perfectly. "Being the hottest girl in the room no longer defines your self-worth or value. Jesus does. He alone made me worth something valuable." I'm excited for you to read the rest. Thank you for picking it up. You're awesome!

Chapter 1

IN THE BEGINNING

If you read this book thoroughly, then it will touch you deeply and help you have the life you deserve! I have been procrastinating about writing this for over 30 years. I have concluded that we all have a book inside us from the hundreds of people I have spoken to. You have a choice to be your story or be the possibility of greatness from your story. This is my story, finally, after 50 years.

Malachi 4:6 says, "**He will turn the hearts of Fathers to their children and the children's hearts back to their fathers. Otherwise, I will come and strike the land with a curse. Our land, our children, and our world have already been struck with a curse.**

The curse is a "Fatherless society," where kids like me grow up believing that somehow it's their fault their dad is gone, or is not present and doesn't love them, or was abandoned or rejected by him. Learn that it is not your fault. You are so loved, so deserving of inner joy; you have no idea!! Through my stories, failures, and successes, you will find yourself and heal that child within you!!

Every human I have encountered has a story. Some are sad, some happy, some boring, and some exhilarating. Please closely examine yourself and think about your journey as you read mine. Get ready to write your book to unlock all that is inside you. True freedom is being able to forgive, accept, repent, embrace, and move forward.

My goal in finally writing this book is to set the captives free. Yes, I know it's a much-quoted Bible verse, but I'm for real. We all need freedom inside our souls to let go of what doesn't serve ourselves or the world positively. My goal is to become raw, honest, and authentic throughout this book, and it would set you free in some tangible way because of my honesty. So, you can go out and set others free and live the life you deserve based on possibility, not on your story of pain.

Why did I buy this book about someone else's life? That's a great inquiry into yourself & inner reflection. There is only one of you; you are created unlike anyone else, and your story is unlike anyone else's. Only you have the power to use what was meant for evil in your own life and use it for good. This story will leave you sad, mad, happy, ecstatic, and hungry for life. **So, let the journey begin!!**

When I was seventeen, my mom and I moved my senior year of High School to Long Island, New York. I had just discovered the news about my dad and still had yet to process everything. I was sitting in my Psychology professor's class during my senior year. He asked us all to write a paper on a dramatic event that changed the course of our life. I had no idea what was inside me until I started writing. I can remember so vividly how fast this paper was written. See, when we talk or write, and honesty and vulnerability are present, there is no effort in storytelling.

I was coming from a place of fear, pain, and confusion. The paper was just my vehicle to express my emotion and pain, which I never could articulate. Please ask yourself this question. What wants to come out of you that is pinned up inside? This is part of the healing journey within you. It will all be worth it if you get anything from this that gives you release and freedom.

Let's call my Psychology teacher Mr. Burns. I went to Half Hollow Hills, East Dix Hills, NY. It took me less than an hour to write five pages. I remember crying and being sad and mad as I was writing. That's how you know it's what you need. A chemical called Serotonin in your brain is released when you unlock memories that are making you stuck. Serotonin is also what's released when you bungee jump. GO FIGURE...

I was so rushed when I wrote it and handed my paper to Mr. Burns that he immediately read it, and tears came from his eyes. I bawled like a baby because I had never really put into words what had happened to me and why we had moved to New York.

I was born in Arkansas. I moved to Memphis, Tennessee, when I was 4. We lived there until we moved to New York. I went to the same school from K-11. An excellent sweet

Christian school called Briar Crest. We got into trouble if we wore clothes above our knees. I had detention every week for just talking in class.

Moving from that innocence to a New York public school during my senior year in high school was a culture shock. I thought I was well-cultured because my Mom took me to the best restaurants in Memphis. She took me on incredible business trips growing up nationwide and exposed me to places like Limelight in New York, a super cool nightclub in the 80s in New York.

I thought I was Miss Somebody and knew it all. Most 16-year-olds think they know it all. I remember knowing I knew nothing; my perspective was so small and sheltered. I was sitting in my third period on a Tuesday. This is my senior year in high school. I moved to New York (Dix Hills specifically) my senior year.

I remember knowing nothing, and my perspective was so small and sheltered. I was sitting in my third period on a Tuesday. This is my senior year in high school. I moved to New York (Dix Hills specifically) my senior year. I heard a siren ring that sounded like a fire drill bell. In Memphis, we had monthly fire drills. That is where you stand up, and in an orderly fashion, you line up. A teacher guides you to your safe spot outside as a class. Those were thrilling in Memphis because we got to leave the prison, also known as our high school.

The teachers were more like dictators there. As I would in Memphis, I stood to my feet and lined up in front of the class. I was so excited because I finally had something in common with this new environment. I stood for what seemed to be an eternity. I looked around, and in my little Southern accent, I asked why everyone wasn't getting up.

I said, "It's a fire drill all. Do you hear right?" The entire class started laughing and looked at me with complete disbelief. I think they couldn't believe there was still innocence in the world like me. The teacher clued me into what the siren was for. He said, "See, sweetie, this Ain't the South or your little country school. This is New York.

What you heard happens regularly because all the druggies go to the back of the school around the third period. Today one of them is not so lucky because that siren means someone overdosed." I was about one foot tall at that moment. I could not believe anything like that really happened in the world.

Now in Memphis, when I would go home to my neighborhood, we had some rougher kids that went to public school. As a single Mom, my mom couldn't afford the fancy neighborhood and private school for me. Our neighborhood was safe, but the kids were wild. I knew about weed from them, so I would smoke with the derelicts as a latchkey when I came home from school. That was the wildest thing I ever knew about or did. Well, sort of. But I'll tell you more in detail later. I hope this paints a picture of who I was and how I was.

When we moved, I was numb. I just wanted to forget all that had happened and start over. That began me running from myself and people-pleasing at an advanced level.

Then Mr. Burns gave me that assignment, and all I had tried to leave behind was still there, locked away in my subconscious, literally eating me up inside. Maybe you have things you are running from that eat you up. Please use my book to inspire you even if no one ever reads your story or what you write to **let it out.**

When I handed my story to Mr. Burns, he cried and told me I was brave. He could not believe that what I wrote was real. He only saw a pretty girl from the South with a cute little accent. Looks are deceiving. I'll tell you that. I learned at a very young age to put on a smile, and as long as I looked good, everything was okay. As my Meme always said, "Never judge a book by its cover".

Unfortunately, my paper is long gone, but I remember most of it. I will start with the article that opened Pandora's box and helped me piece so many portions together that were a mystery to me growing up. In one article in the paper, everything from six years old to sixteen made sense. I woke up to this in the Arkansas paper when I went home for Thanksgiving at almost sixteen years old. This was England, Arkansas, a little town.

My entire family still lived there, but my Mom and I no longer do. You better believe our phone was ringing first thing. The first paragraph kind of tells you all. I believed my Dad was dead for most of my life up to this point. As I said earlier, I was raised by a single Mom with no siblings. This is what that paper said that I wrote over thirty years ago. It was called "The Dramatic Event."

Betzner arrested in Florida by Federal Narcotics Agents Tuesday

Gary Wayne Betzner, a former Hazen resident who supposedly jumped from the White River Bridge in Des Arc in 1977, was arrested by federal drug enforcement officials at Gainesville, Florida Tuesday afternoon, November 20.

Betzner is now in the custody of the U. S. Marshal at Jacksonville, Florida and being held without bond. At the time of his arrest, he had approximately 400 pounds of cocaine in his possession. Officials were unable to even estimate the street value of the drug.

Sheriff Dale Madden was notified by the Federal Bureau of Investigation last Tuesday that Betzner was in custody. He is being sought by Prairie County officials for possession of a controlled substance with intent to deliver and also with intent to manufacture. The charges stemmed from a raid by police authorities on his home in Hazen on September 9, 1977. He was arrested and released on $15,000 bond pending plea day proceedings at DeValls Bluff on September 19 in Circuit Court. The night before the hearing, he stopped on the bridge at Des Arc about midnight, handed his wife a note purportedly suicidal, and disappeared.

Betzner had previously been indicted by a federal grand jury in Philadelphia in May of that year along with five others. The indictment charged conspiracy to distribute cocaine. He was scheduled to stand trial on those charges in Miami, Florida on October 3, 1977.

A federal warrant for his arrest by the Federal Bureau of Investigation was issued on October 18, 1977 on grounds of unlawful flight to avoid prosecution after dragging and searching operations on the White River failed to turn up his body.

If I had a book by someone who had an experience of not having a Dad in their life back then, I would have been able to process my feelings much better. I will explain these emotions that are sometimes still there throughout this book. Here's the gist of the paper. When I was six months old, my parents got divorced. My Mom lived in Arkansas, and being a divorced woman with a child in the early 70s was taboo. My Dad was abusive to my Mom and had a series of affairs. So she left with no money in her pocket. My Mom immediately found a tiny apartment in Little

Rock, the closest big city to her, and within four days, she had a nanny to help her with me so she could work. Mom told me that sometimes she had not to eat so I could. She was struggling.

At age four, my Mom's best friend (Mimi) son had a brilliant idea to start an overnight delivery service. It was called Federal Express. So Esther (my Mom) started her career. What an opportunity she had. See, in the 70s, there were no rules for sexual harassment in the workplace.

She had to take much crap to keep her previous jobs, but she knew she was safe once Fed Express came along. If she worked hard and did a good job, she could go far and always provide for me. My Mom never forgot the pain of what she was rescued from, which helped drive her to be such a great businesswoman.

At around five, we moved to Memphis, where Federal Express relocated too. My Mom was starting to make more money, and we were finally not broke. My Dad remarried the woman he cheated on my Mom with and had two more kids with her—the oldest, only two years younger than me. So do the math. Six months after my Mom left him, his mistress was pregnant.

After the divorce, I saw my Dad rarely, like when he could fit me in. My Mom was super protective of me because she knew how he was. I only remember visiting his new family's house when I was four. My Dad was a crop duster, and he married a woman that was a trust fund brat. They lived in a lovely home with a pool and a nanny. My half-siblings were two and a newborn at that time. This is my memory of that experience. My Dad went to work, and I was stuck with the stepmom and kids. The maid cooked a fantastic breakfast, which I was used to at my Memes house in England, Arkansas. I remember she gave my little brother a plate. It was an egg, a piece of bacon, and a homemade biscuit. I sat at the table waiting for mine. Remember, I was only four. I asked, "Can I have some too?" The step monster looked at me and said no. I don't want to be embarrassed if you turn out fat like the rest of your family.

So the nanny gave me strawberry yogurt, which was rotten. I didn't eat it even though I was hungry. To this day, I still can't eat strawberry yogurt. That was the beginning of my relationship with food and body image. (This is my 50-year-old self-talk, not my 16-year-old self that wrote the paper.)

The next time I saw my Dad, he took me flying in his plane, and we made loops. I was four. That means I was in the open cockpit of an airplane, and he did tremendous force thrusting loops with me strapped in my seat in front of him. I remember telling him he was stupid when we returned to his house. I don't know why I said that. He took out a belt and spanked me, and told me never to say that again to him. That was the last time my Mom ever let me return there. He did send me a little black and white

TV that year. He sent me home with a little pink sleeping bag with a matching pillow. I should have known I had Daddy issues early.

I remember nights sitting up watching that 9-inch black and white TV under the covers in my room. I even had a big color TV in my room, but I still watched that TV because it came from my Dad. I carried that little pillow from the sleeping bag until I was fourteen. Without it, I couldn't go to anyone's house to sleep over for ten years. It was the only tangible thing I had to hold onto from my Dad. Now I know those things were my security blanket of feeling like maybe my Dad really loved me.

He would visit periodically in Memphis but much less frequently. I have two distinct memories of him visiting until the big day at age six. The first was when he visited our little townhouse in an Aspen wood complex. He wanted to put me to bed, and he was walking up the stairs and lit a joint.

In 1975, My Mom asked, "What are you doing?" as he blew pot smoke in my face. He said I'm enlightening our daughter. So Esther said, "Don't you ever do that around my daughter again." She kicked him out. Looking back at age 50, I held much anger for my Mom for asking him to leave, as if that's why he wasn't in my life much.

As children, we tend to blame the parent that sticks it out. We are so mortified of losing a morsel of the crumbs we get from the absent parent we stay in denial about the truth. Often to cover up the pain and feelings of inadequacy, we feel of not being enough for the absent parent to stick around.

The next time I remember seeing my Dad, I was 6 six. My Mom had just bought a fantastic townhouse. She was really doing it but still struggling with no child support from my Dad. She would instead work her butt off than go to court and demand child support and then have to deal with my Dad coming around. (I Held my Mom hostage over that too).

So this time, my Mom woke me up around 11 at night. I had on a little pink nightgown. You know, the one most of us have if we are 40 plus. The gown with a little ruffle collar around the neckline and pink polyester. My hair was in little pink foam curlers. She got me up, put me on the little rest next to her driver's seat, and drove off in our brown Oldsmobile LTD. I asked her what we were doing. She answered, "We will see your Daddy to get some money."

I distinctly remember thinking, "Wow, it's dark. And where is my Dad this late?" We pulled up on the runway at the local airport. My Mom said, "Stay here, honey Mommy has to get some money, so we will be okay for a while. I asked if I could come, and she said no. This was between her and my Dad.

As my Dad's plane pulled up, he got out in a fur coat, a Rolex watch, and a fresh '70s perm. I looked at him and waved from about 50 yards away. He waved back and smiled. My Mom looked over and held her finger up as if I would be right there.

My Dad got back on the plane, and my Mom returned to the car. As she got in the car, I asked her if we would be okay. My Dad gave her the child support he promised but had never given any in 5 years. The amount was less than $2,000.

In that instant, I knew I wasn't important to him. Later in life, I realized that nothing was important to him that really mattered. Looking back at age fifty, I wish I had seen him as selfish. Here my Mom has to take me to daycare, leaving me there. Sometimes I was the last one to be picked up because, as a woman in the 70s, you worked harder than men to prove your worth.

Here's my Dad with a $10,000 Rolex, a $20,000 fur, and his own private plane; wow. To think I made it about me not being enough for so many years. That was the last time I saw my Dad until I was almost 16. On the morning of my 7th birthday, I woke up to rain pouring outside. Our Pastor from Southland Baptist Church in Memphis, Tennessee, was knocking on our door. I remember thinking how cool he was there for my birthday. I had also given my life to Jesus a few months before, so I thought that made us BFFs (Best Friends Forever).

That, unfortunately, wasn't what he was there for at all. My Mom asked me to sit on the sofa. We had the most incredible tan L-shaped fur sofa. He sat beside me, put his hand on my knee, and said, "Sweetie, I'm not here for your birthday. I'm so sorry. I'm here to tell you your Daddy committed suicide."

I asked, "What does that mean?" He said, "Your Daddy jumped off the White River Bridge this morning in Arkansas, and he's dead." Everything became slow motion. I looked at him and barely shed a tear and said, "Okay, Thank you for being here," or something like that. That was the nail in the coffin of being a people pleaser and living dual lives. I went upstairs and started playing with my Barbies.

I played for what seemed like days. My Mom would check on me to ensure I was okay. I don't remember eating or anything. I immersed myself in another world I could control with my Barbies. At least in that little doll house my Mom handmade for me, I could control what happened. It was a beautiful, two-level house and had four bedrooms. She made carpet for each room and handmade little curtains. It was amazing.

They drug the river for my Dad's body for days and never found it. I wondered if maybe the angels already took him to heaven, which was why they couldn't find his body. My Mom kept on working. I kept going to school, and life went on. I was a single Mom's daughter, but my Dad was dead.

So, somehow in the 70s, it was taboo to be a single Mom's kid. Especially when I went to a private school where all the rich kid's parents were all still married. I could have said, "My Mom's single because my dad killed himself." But somehow, saying she was divorced was better than being shunned.

My Dad had a brother, Uncle Louis. Louis lived in another state, but periodically he would come and visit and bring me little gifts. I now know he was checking on me. I remember we were at Wendy's for dinner when I was around thirteen.

We loved to go to Wendy's, just Mom and I. She had to work till well after 5:30 many nights and was too pooped to cook. I loved getting my cheeseburger with mustard and a Dr. Pepper and was happy.

This time was different. I had a terrible cough, and these two men there kept asking if I was okay. Esther didn't think much of it until they arrived at our house a few weeks later. The doorbell rang, and the two men from Wendy's were wearing long black coats. My Mom was scared. She didn't know how they found us.

She asked how they found us, and they said they were so worried about me that they took down our license plate and found us. This was way before the internet. They wanted to see me to see if I was okay and wanted pictures of me.

My Mom promptly asked who sent them and asked them to leave. We never saw them again. Later we found out they were from the cartel. There was another time there was a kidnapping threat at my high school for me. I remember being sent to the principal's office and waiting until the coast was clear. I still thought my Dad was dead, and I never knew all of this because he was still alive.

My whole family lived in England, Arkansas, and word spread fast there. When I woke up Thanksgiving right after I turned fifteen, the article was on the previous pages. Okay, go ahead and turn back and read it. It will put my whole story into perspective. Gary Wayne Betzner was indicted for possessing 1,000 kilos of cocaine in Lake City, Florida. Now it all made sense that he was alive. That's why nobody was in the river when they drugged it for days. That's why my Uncle came to buy me gifts and wanted to hang out. That's why those two weird men wanted a picture of me.

My Dad was a major drug smuggler and was directly involved with the Iran Contra Scandal. I'll tell you all about in the following chapters and his crazy life while my Mom was raising me. All of this was the foundation of how I started to process my feelings about myself. I have spent over 40 years trying to put that little girl back together, and through this journey in this book, you will see me finally loving myself!

I am the possibility for all wounded hearts by their earthly Father to know they are loved at the most profound and highest level. Whatever happened to you that made you feel rejected, abandoned, or unloved as a child is not your fault. You are so loved, so deserving of inner joy you have no idea!! Through my stories, failures, and successes, you will find and heal that child within you!!

Every human I have encountered has a story. Some are sad, some happy, some boring, and some exhilarating. Please closely examine yourself and think about your journey as you read mine. Then get ready to write your book to unlock everything inside you. True freedom is being able to forgive, accept, repent, embrace, and move forward.

My goal in finally writing this book is to set the captives free. Yes, I know it's a much-quoted Bible verse, but I'm for real. We all need freedom inside our souls to let go of what doesn't serve ourselves or the world positively. My goal is to become raw, honest, and authentic throughout this book, and it would set you free in some tangible way because of my honesty. So you can go out and set others free and live the life you deserve based on possibility, not on your story of pain.

Chapter 2

HISTORY REPEATS ITSELF

Now that you know why I wanted to write this book, I can fill in all the blanks. My Dad was born into a generational curse that he seemed not to break the cycle of. See, that tends to happen until you see who you are and why you were created. The how or why you are the way you are and how the evil or bad that happened growing up was never meant to define you.

I took everything personally and decided at a young age that it had to be my fault that my Dad left and didn't really love me the way a Dad is supposed to love a child. This created a hole in my being that I spent years trying to fill.

Until I understood his lack of love or leaving had nothing to do with me. It had everything to do with his inability to reflect upon his past and become a better person.

I was blessed to have a Mom who always encouraged therapy when I was younger. It literally took until my new sister came along for me to figure out this self-doubt I had been carrying wasn't because I wasn't enough. It was mainly because of the lack of love and protection I felt as a child and an adult from my father. She showed me a narcissist couldn't really have the capacity to love anyone more significant than themselves. His lack of love had nothing to do with me. He didn't leave me until I finally got the actual distinction that my Dad had just left. He didn't just leave me.

I'LL SAY IT AGAIN, AND THOSE OF YOU THAT BOUGHT THIS FOR YOUR OWN HEALING, WRITE THIS ON A CARD ALL OVER YOUR HOUSE!!

MY DAD JUST LEFT; HE DIDN'T LEAVE ME!!!!

In another chapter, I'll tell you about my four new siblings I never knew about until ancestry DNA. That's who I am talking about. Her name is Malibu. What a blessing God gave me in her. She has truly helped me see the light. What a gift a sister from the same Mr. LOL!!

I have tried to piece my Dad's childhood together, but I only have bits and pieces from different people in his family. My Grandmother Pauline was a tall woman. She was a socialite and a wonderful person, from what I heard. Pauline married a man named Zenard. He worked at Sears and Roebuck General Store and was abusive to her and the two boys they had together.

My Dad has a younger brother. His name is, let's say Louis. He was five years younger than Dad. Dad was always the tough one. I heard a story about my father when he was around six. He hid a miniature baseball bat behind the door. He knew his Dad was going to beat his Mom. So he waited to hit him on the back of the head and take up for his Mom. After Zenard beat the crap out of his wife, Dad went to hit him at six years old. His Dad, of course, caught him and beat him senselessly to teach him his place.

The abuse was so bad that my Dad has no recollection of this ever happening. It was so significant I'm sure there were broken bones. My uncle says he remembers hiding under the house at two years old and could hear the screaming. He stayed under there until nightfall so it wouldn't happen to him too. I can only imagine how scary that must have been for a baby to hide under a damp, cold house alone.

I believe seeing all that abuse and being helpless was the beginning of Dad's disassociation from his feelings. Thus the birth of a narcissist. The definition of a narcissist is **"narcissist: a person who thinks the world revolves around them"** I feel he took on that it was his fault his Mom was being abused and he was too weak to protect her. He felt rejected by his father at a deep level and had no safe space to explore why within himself. Whether your Dad beat you, wasn't there emotionally, or was physically absent, we all create different coping mechanisms to survive. Until we finally realize that we have a Father in heaven who loves us unconditionally and never goes anywhere!!

Pauline and Zenard divorced shortly after. She took the boys to live with their grandparents. My uncle explained that he loved it there and that he felt safe. They lived there for about three years. Their ages were ten (my Dad) and five). Her parents were married and owned a farm. They were simple folk, is what I hear, and totally salt of the earth. They owned chickens and cows and killed a pig yearly for its winter meat. My Nanu was 16, and her hubby was thirty-two when they married. I puked in my mouth when I heard that because that seemed so gross!

Then I thought of the time frame. This was back in the late 1800s. Things were way different back then. Who am I to judge? They stayed married for over 50 years and raised a fantastic woman (my Grandma).
He was a guard at the rock quarry. When they first got married, and he was also a poker player.

One morning, after they first married, he left in an empty wagon and was gone for two weeks. When he came home, he arrived with a wagon full of furniture for his new bride. They moved into their new home together and started their lives. That's all I really knew about them. They lived there until my Dad was around ten or eleven, and then she remarried.

My grandmother married a man named Bob. He was much older than her and was very successful. He owned a working 4000-acre farm. I never met my grandmother, but my Mom told me she was a great artist and quite the socialite. In the 50s, to get divorced as a woman must have been terrifying. Only a few women worked outside the home. She was in her 20s, divorced with two small boys in Arkansas. I'm sure that must have been trying and scary. When she married Bob, she loved him, but she knew he could stabilize the boys.

My Dad told me one of his memories was a conversation he heard between his Mom and step Dad. He said, "They aren't blood, but I'll take care of them because they're yours. I want to have my own kids with you." The cycle of rejection continued for my Dad from yet another father. This one might not have beaten him physically, but I'm sure that must have hurt him mentally.

Bob and Pauline had two boys together. Their names were, let's say to keep everyone a little anonymous here, Fred (he is now deceased) and the other Peter. Peter later took over his Dad's farm because Bob always said, "Blood's thicker than water, and you two boys aren't my real boys because I have sons now."

The younger one, Fred, my Mom tells me, was terrific. He was super musical and fun. He was the most like his Mom. He was constantly being social and super outgoing. He was about ten years younger than Dad.

While my Mom was pregnant with me, Fred jumped out of a boat into a shallow lake. He didn't know how deep the water was and broke his neck.

My Mom sat at the hospital when she was pregnant with me daily. She loved Fred. Her marriage to Dad was already so rocky, but she found peace by being at the hospital. She said her water broke at the hospital with me. I had the umbilical cord wrapped around my neck when I was born. She said it was because she sat in that hospital chair daily, hoping Fred would recover. He never did. He died shortly after.

This was Dad's second death in one year. I'm sure that added to his lack of capacity for real love for a child because he never learned real coping skills. Then, in November, the month I was conceived, my Grandmother Pauline died in a car crash. She was driving to deliver a pie to someone for Thanksgiving, and she hit a rain puddle. The car hydroplaned into a ditch, and she was killed instantly.

My Mom and Dad moved into the big house right after Pauline died, and they were living in the trailer at Hazen. Right after she died within days, my Dad went crazy. He went home to my Mom and said, "We have to get pregnant. I want to have a baby and name her after my Mom. Yes, my real name is Pauline."

The story goes like this. My Dad had already been cheating on my Mom. She was ready to leave him, but he insisted on getting her pregnant. This was to ease his pain about his Mom and brother's death. That's what a narcissist does, always thinking about what will help them. Not realizing my Mom had lost two people that she also loved dearly. Not a reason to have a baby, but that's how their minds worked.

I know this all goes back to how he was raised. He was never put first when he was young. The dads had never prioritized his emotional well-being, so he learned to be selfish early on. I am not making excuses for his behavior. Trust me, I put him on an unworthy pedestal for years. Once I went through years of anger, sadness, and rejection, I finally let God lead me to real forgiveness and peace.

My revelation of all of this has helped me heal my soul. When I was conceived, my Dad turned my Mom upside down and held her by her feet. He said he wanted to ensure it all got to the egg. What a nut, and my poor Mom. So, 9.5 months later, I was born. I was conceived in his Mom's bed at her house. They stayed at the big house, as it was called, for a while after Grandma died. I can only imagine the happiness and resentment my Mom must have felt. She was still so innocent and knew she wanted out, but she also wanted a Li'l sidekick (AKA me) to be with her on her journey. Their marriage was rocky from the beginning. So it's time to tell you their drama so you can get a little deeper into the psychology of my thoughts. In the next chapter, I will tell you my Mom's sweet and sad story of why she would marry a man like my Dad in the first place. They say love is blind, but so is pain until it's not.

They were introduced by a good friend of my Mom's in Arkansas. Dad was super good-looking. He had perfectly combed light brown hair and beautiful hazel eyes and could charm the pants off anyone. Now that I have met all these new siblings, he charmed many panties off over the years before my Mom. He was 6-5 and a successful pilot. In the county where he lived, he was a Mason Shriner and a Congress Chairperson to Senator Dale Bumpers. For a small-town girl, he appeared to be so savvy.

On one of their first dates, he took my Mom flying. When my Mom was little, she lived on a farm outside of Woodson, Arkansas. She used to lay on her back in the cotton fields and watch planes fly over. She told me she would think about where those people were going and what was their life like? A little farm girl was dreaming of a better life. This was the beginning of her love affair with aviation. She wanted to go anywhere other than where she was.

When she and Gary met, she was still living in England, Arkansas, living with her parents. She was the manager at the local Kroger Market. I've always heard that she was excellent with numbers and projections for growth for the store. Her business mindset was already impeccable. This was something my Dad found very appealing. He knew she would make a great partner for his business and could keep the books and the business running flawlessly.

Initially, his thoughts weren't about her being gorgeous or how much he liked her as a girlfriend but what she could do for him. Any truly successful marriage is always about service to the other person. From the beginning, this relationship was doomed. Hindsight is always 20/20! Thank God she didn't know then what she knew later, or I wouldn't be here writing this book that I pray helps millions.

They went on a few dates. Then on one of their dates, my Mom said no to sex with him, but he forced himself on her. Back then, this kind of thing was not talked about. If you had much shame as a woman from unresolved issues, you would blame yourself for such unthinkable acts. That is exactly what my Mom did. She blamed herself for not being strong enough to say no. She buried the pain inside her, told no one, and broke up with him.

She started dating other people right after they stopped seeing each other. She started dating a man right after she ended it with my Dad. She got engaged to him shortly after they started dating. He was studying in Little Rock to be a doctor. He was from Iran. He was crazy about my Mom from the beginning. After a few months of dating, he proposed. My Mom reluctantly said yes. She thought this was way better than Gary, to finally get out of my small town. It was two weeks before she was going to marry this guy; my Dad showed up. It never occurred to her that she didn't have to do either. She could have waited on plan C!

If you are currently in a toxic relationship, please take some time to heal before you date anyone. Ask yourself some simple questions. What made me pick a person who didn't treat me the best? Start reflecting and dig inside yourself so you don't do what my sweet Momma thought was her only option. SETTLE!

Dad had watched "The Graduate", the movie, and after he saw it, he knew he couldn't let my Mom go. He called her parents and said you must let me talk to your daughter. She can't marry this other guy. So she talked to him late that night. He told her I'm coming to get you early in the morning and bring your toothbrush and a gown. Even though she was thinking about what I was doing in her mind, she kept moving forward. So she did just that. Pack her toothbrush and her gown in her purse.

The following day, he showed up and told her parents, "I am taking your daughter to Oklahoma to get married whether I have your blessing or not." So they left and went to the apartment she and her fiancé were about to move into together after the wedding. They pulled into the complex's driveway, and my Mom went in alone. She knew her fiancé was at school and he wouldn't be there so she could leave the note and ring. She left her ring and a note and said how sorry she was and left.

I often wonder what happened to him. I asked my Mom if he had tried to see her. Right after she left the note, he got home. She and Dad had already left the state. He went to my Grandparent's house trying to stop her. He even contacted the Arkansas state police to put up roadblocks to stop them.

My Dad, a pilot, flew her to Oklahoma right after they left, leaving the note and the ring, which was a lost cause. I often wonder if she would have married him if I had gorgeous skin and dark, thick hair like the Kardashians LOL!

They left that day and got married in Oklahoma. After they were married, he started to control my Mom and all her moves. They first moved to a trailer at his hangar in the middle of nowhere, where his business was for crop dusting. He would leave my Mom alone out there all day. This is all before cell phones or the internet.

My Mom worked for years at Kroger to save enough money to buy her dream car. Right before they got together, she had her car. She bought a forest green 65

Mustang hatchback. Right after they got married, they went to different car dealerships. My Mom would ask, "Why are we selling my car instead of yours?"

He didn't care that she loved that car and that it was her dream. He talked her into selling it to pay off the debts he had incurred before they were married. She was awestruck and wanted to be a good wife, so she went along with it even though it tore her up inside.

He began the cycle of abuse from the beginning. Isolation is always a key component in breaking you down from an abuser. He would make small digs at her appearance and make fun of how she looked. She still has problems with loving herself the way she is, which was almost 50 years ago.

My Mom was very insecure already. Getting boobs at age eleven and always being ginger in a small town can surely poke at your self-esteem. What abusers do is make you feel like you could never get any better than this. So they tear your self-esteem brick by brick until you have nothing left and walk all over you.

She was pregnant with me after six months of being married. She told me several times that he would come at her and tell her to get rid of me. One of the women he cheated on her with was a trust fund brat from the next town over. She knew my Mom was pregnant, and she and my Mom's best friend, who was having sex with my Dad, would tell him to have her get an abortion. How terrible my Mom was isolated on this runway in a trailer in the middle of Bumble Egypt, and her one best friend was sleeping with her husband; wow! After I was born, my Mom was done. It just took her a few worse scenes to go. I have done years of therapy. One exercise I did was being brought back to my earliest childhood memory.

I remembered the brown shag carpet, and wood panels on the walls. The sheets in my crib were pink, and I was so scared in bed. That is the night when she had enough. They fought when he got home because she finally confronted him about cheating. He denied it and started hitting her.

At that point, he threatened to take me away from her, and she would never see me again. She got in my room, got me out of bed, and propped herself against the door so he couldn't get in all night, holding me tight. I remember that, and I was only nine months old!

Some people don't believe you can remember that far, but I did. Your cellular structure in your brain can get what I call bruises from trauma. This imprint in your mind leads you to people and places you know aren't good for you but familiar. Until you genuinely heal the past by seeing where all the pieces in your life came from and why. Then you can start to heal the bruises and truly have beauty for ashes. You can help others avoid making the same mistakes you made based on not correctly filing your past where it belongs. It doesn't have to define you.

From that night forward, she planned her escape. The final straw was when my Mom left for the weekend with me to visit her parents. When she returned, my aunt called and told her my Dad's car was parked outside a hotel in town all weekend with the trust fund lady. That was it. My Mom was done. You'll know when you're sick and tired of being sick and tired.

The next day when Dad had to go crop-dusting for the day, she packed the crappy little car she had to settle for. She took me and what little she had to a friend's house till she could get a job. She didn't go home because of all her bruises. That was the beginning of just me and Esther.

Chapter 3

THE GRANDPARENTS!
MEME AND PAPA

How do I even explain my Mom? You know what? She deserves her own chapter. I will lay the foundation of how she became who she is in the next chapter. I wrote a story called "Guilt, Sex, and My Little Child" when I went to Orange Coast College in 1987.

It was also the first time I wrote about my Mom's history and my history of abuse that I had tucked away for years. In a psychology paper, I only talked about what happened with my Dad when I was seventeen in New York.

There's a pattern. I could only put on paper what I felt and could not express in words to another person. When I wrote, I could say everything I felt and had inside without being vulnerable in front of someone else.

Now I'm older, and I don't care as much. I don't have shame anymore. I know this book has taken so long because of all my experiences, so they could all come together for you. I procrastinated for years, thinking this story didn't matter.

My Meme, "The 2nd Most Amazing Woman in the World," my Mom's Mom had a sad past. There are many repeat patterns throughout my story, this being one of them. If you breathe right now, get a snack or a coffee, take a moment, and think about your own life. Do you have repeat patterns? Start the inquiry of where it starts. What was the root or the beginning of a pattern that was a setup for you not to have the life God promised you?

We were created to be fruitful and joyous and to have abundance. Like when you make soup, it tastes bland and gross unless you start with a great stock. We all are great stock! We are sons and daughters of the Creator of the universe! Sometimes we just had rotten veggies put in our stock—those we have to root out of our life literally. So the soup, AKA our life, can be how it was intended to be. That's what I want for you, is a beautiful life, but first, we will do some digging, so you can get rid of what's in your life that doesn't serve you for the life you were designed to have from the beginning. My Mom's side was the best stock!

Okay, back to my Meme. My Grandmother was born in Mississippi. She was a daughter of a railroad worker. He was a hardworking man but was gone a lot. I guess they had much making up for lost time together hence nine kids, and she was the youngest of the nine. Her Mother died when she was 2. The Dad was overwhelmed with so many kids and couldn't take care of her and her older brother, who was four. So, he put them both in a state-run orphanage and paid every month so they could stay and not get adopted. She was there till she was four, a little over two years.

Her Dad ran an ad in the newspaper for a bride. His ad read, "Needed: a bride to help raise my young children. Home will be supplied for you and your children in exchange for child rearing and running a household.' Miss Nancy was the mail-order bride's name. She had two daughters of her own that she brought into the marriage. By this time, Meme was almost five; her oldest sibling was twenty-six and had already moved. There were five at home, three of his and two of hers.

Meme was the only girl from my Great Grandpas' side. Right after they were married, he started working on the RR again, and Meme was home with a woman she barely knew. Over the years, I gathered that she was treated like Nelly Olson treated sweet Laura Ingles from Little House on the Prairie. From such a young age, Meme adopted an orphan spirit. An orphan spirit is something that many people struggle with, both in the Body of Christ, as well as in the world.

When Adam and Eve chose to disobey God in the Garden, sin entered the world. Unfortunately, that disobedience caused a separation between God and man. We've all heard of separation anxiety. It is a real thing. When a baby is separated from its parents, it often experiences great fear. This is a normal reaction when those they have known as protectors are no longer with them.

So, too, when man chose to turn their back on God, an unexpected fear entered their life. Their protector and provider appeared to have left their presence.

The thing we must know about God is that He is merciful. So often, when we have done something wrong, we take the way of Adam and Eve and recoil—isolating ourselves from God and others. We feel alienated and alone. But the opposite is true. God never leaves us. We leave Him.
God is a gentleman. He will never violate our decisions, even when they may go against His greatest desire—to draw near to us. When a wrong decision is made, knowing He is quick to forgive if we only come to Him is good.

There is something unique about a father's role in a child's life. The father and child relationship is the heart of where our identity is formed, and it should be a healthy picture of how our Heavenly Father interacts with us.

A deep void is created when one is abandoned or rejected by their earthly Father. This often makes it difficult for us to interact with God or others. Our trust has been broken, and healing must take place.

Knowing the Father's love is crucial for anyone functioning as a healthy human!!

What does an orphan spirit look like?

"A type of demonic Spirit that invades a person's mind causing a sense of abandonment, loneliness, alienation, and isolation. It often attaches itself to someone who has experienced extreme rejection in their life. A person operating out of an orphan spirit compensates for these feelings of insecurity by being performance-driven, competitive, and working independently. Per struggle with self-worth and find it difficult to maintain healthy relationships."

We often live with dysfunction for so long in our lives that we don't realize we are struggling.

Ask yourself these questions...

- **Do I operate out of insecurity?**
- **Am I jealous of others' successes?**
- **Do I serve God to earn His love?**
- **Do I self-medicate by pulling deeply inward?**
- **Do I struggle with self-worth?**
- **Do I fill the void by constantly working, through physical gratification, or with narcissistic behavior or self-indulgence?**
- **Am I driven by the need to succeed?**
- **Do I use people to accomplish my goals?**

- Do I repel my biological or spiritual children?
- Do I struggle with anger or fits of rage?
- Am I always in competition with others?
- Do I lack self-esteem?
- Do I receive my identity from material possessions, physical appearance, or activities?

If you've answered yes to several of these, it's safe to say that there may be a heart issue that deeply needs healing.

You see, the opposite of one abandoned is one adopted. Adoption is a wonderful thing.

When a child is adopted, they are no longer penniless. They are no longer without a name. In the best of scenarios, they are given an identity through a new family—where they will be loved and appreciated.
Often, in cases of adoption, the family they are given provides much better care than the original parents ever could.

When we are operating in the Spirit of adoption...

- We are secure
- We celebrate the accomplishments of others
- We experience acceptance
- We fill emotional voids with intimate time with the Father
- We allow the Spirit to lead us into our calling

- We serve others and provide opportunities for them to grow in their destiny in Christ
- We don't use anger or other forms of manipulation to get our way
- We bless others around us, freely sharing the Father's love with others
- We love ourselves and exhibit healthy self-esteem
- We are grounded in our identity in Christ

How do I get healing from something that has controlled my life for so long?

The first step to healing is admitting that there's a problem in the first place.

Pray this prayer with me:

"Father, I admit that I am struggling to connect with You in a healthy way because of the rejection I've experienced in my past. I ask You to forgive me for assuming that You were like the human beings who have hurt me, and I ask You to help me start the process of healing that I so desperately need. I give You permission to begin cleaning out the things in my life that hold me back from truly getting my identity from a Heavenly Father who loves me unconditionally, in the name of Yeshua, Amen."

https://www.curtlandry.com/is-the-orphan-spirit-operating-in- my-life/#.Xol8qm5FxMs

This beautiful article published by such a sweet ministry, Curt Landry Ministries, hits the nail on the head about an orphan spirit. So, my sweet Meme operated her whole life in the orphan spirit herself. Meme always felt like something was wrong with her. When her Dad left for his job, and Nancy barely paid attention to her, she just gave her the essentials and loved on her own daughters. This went on her whole home life until she married my Papa at sixteen. From an early age, she was literally in an orphanage. Then he married a woman who continued that neglect, and inside she felt she wasn't enough.

Meme was always about the family she created. Papa was a farmer, and they lived in a little farmhouse in Woodson on four hundred acres that Papa farmed. They were super poor. My Mom said they didn't even have indoor plumbing. Meme gave birth to all four kids at home. That orphan spirit dominated her. She was always cooking and cleaning and never taking time for herself. She was super clean and a great cook. Her entire life was about service to her family. Which, yes, this sounds perfect. It's called balance.

When My Mom was sixteen, they moved to an up-and-coming town in Arkansas called England. My Papa saw the future, and it was fast food. So he built a Dairy Delight like Dairy Queen. Momma and her little brother worked there.

This was the first time my Mom had her own room and indoor plumbing.

Most of my memories are of this cute little town and that house. England is a town twenty minutes south of Little Rock, but it could have been two hours because it is so rural. England had its own culture, for sure. There was one light in town.

The entire town, from the Dairy Delight to the mini-mart, was about five minutes driving 30mph. The town was mainly built on farming and agriculture. Most of the people drove trucks and had acreage as their homes. Hunting was a way of life for many of them.

When I would come there, I was the city girl coming to town like an anomaly. On the weekend, all the young people would ride uptown and do what's called the loop. See, we didn't have cell phones or the internet. We knew the best way to discover what was happening was to drive uptown and make a loop. The minute you would see someone you know, you would wave or flash your lights, and they would pull over.

I started driving around the age of thirteen. This town was a little lenient on permits. LOL, I have many memories of going to England throughout my childhood. I couldn't wait to get there and call my friends when I got into town so they could take me on a loop. One memory I have was I was riding uptown with my cousin, and she knew a bootlegger in town.

See, England is what you would call "A dry county," which means no liquor. The closest liquor store was ten miles away. So we drove to his house and flashed our lights. I was fourteen or fifteen, and he brought out a case of malt duck. Oh my, it tastes like fruity throw-up, but I didn't care.

We went to the cemetery to drink because it was quiet out there, and our family had a large plot for us to be buried one day. This was before anybody had died yet. So our plot was empty. Almost all my family, including my sweet cousin Laura is buried there. In the South, people prepare for death early, and my Grandparents wanted all of us to be together even in death. Pretty sweet, actually.

After we got tore up, we found out there was a party at the river. We went, and the next thing I knew, we were night skiing on the river. This was one of the dumbest things I did as a kid. Thank the Lord, nothing happened because this river had alligators and snakes. God always protected me even though I sure didn't deserve it.

I still love that little town even though my whole family, kids, hubby, and Mom are all in California. I still think of that house as home even though it was sold after my Papa died over ten years ago. When I was a hippie and on The Grateful Dead tour in the 80s, I always gave everyone that address and their number because I knew they would live there till they died.

That was the home of many of my childhood memories with my family. They lived there for over fifty years. It was on about half an acre with a large backyard. My Papa would plant a big garden every year on Good Friday. He would have corn, peppers, tomatoes, watermelon, squash, and green beans, which was awesome.

The only super gross thing was the mosquitos. They would come in swarms and eat me up. I was so allergic. We had three average size bedrooms and one bathroom inside the home. This got interesting when the whole family was there during every major holiday; about seventeen people were there. The den and kitchen were connected, and the dining table could seat ten comfortably.

Every Christmas and Thanksgiving till I was well into my 20s, my cousins and I had to sit at the kid's table in the other room. That's pretty funny. There was a hierarchy of adults to us kids even though we were adults. Their house was precisely three walking minutes and one block to the Dairy Delight, which my Papa drove every day and barely ever walked lol...

Growing up, my Mom said Meme never rested. She was always cooking or cleaning or doing for her kids. All of her kids stayed close to her. My Aunt Lois moved right around the corner, and both of her boys moved about a mile away next door to each other. She never felt love from her own family, so she created a very tight-knit family. That's amazing for someone who didn't have that role model.

Mom and I lived in Arkansas till I was almost five, and then we moved two hours away. We came home almost every weekend. I spent many summers in Arkansas because my Mom had to work a lot. She was working for Federal Express and climbing the corporate ladder. So in the summers, finding childcare took much work.

My Mom was finally living part of her dream; she was flying all over on business trips for Federal Express. I spent every Thanksgiving and every Christmas at Meme and Papas until I was in my 30s.

My Mom would load up Santa Claus and drive it to Arkansas. Every Christmas morning my whole life until I had kids, and even a few years later, I woke up to Santa at 504 NE first street. I knew it was time to get up because I could smell sausage gravy and biscuits. I had "Santa" till I was in my 20s, lol.

Every Black Friday, my cousins, I, and all my family would go shopping. My Grandmother kept a perfect home with great food and worked at the Dairy Delight. She did all of it so she could buy what she wanted to buy for everyone for Christmas. This was the one time I saw her so happy when she had that Christmas list and her kids together to go shopping.

There was a cute little hot dog place at the mall called Mr. Dunderbachs. Every Black Friday, we would go there. She would get a beer, which was a huge deal for her. I would get so tickled because there was an upstairs, and we would go up there and put all our shopping bags down and eat our pretzels, and she would have a beer, right after she would laugh the sweetest laugh and say, "Polly I feel woozy help me down those stairs." I can still see her sweet face. My grandparents loved the Lord. Meme still felt a little guilty about drinking, so she didn't do it too often.

I notice that I do a lot for people, not always just because I love them but also out of a place of feeling like they will love me and never leave if I do. I know now that people love me no matter what I do or don't do. I wish I could have told my Meme that.

Your house doesn't have to be perfect, and you don't have to cook all the time. She did everything to show us her love. Also, part of that orphan spirit is always trying to make sure people know how much they are loved partially so they never leave too.

Even though she knew her Father loved her, she still took on a self-image that she wasn't enough, just as she was, and that she needed to do something special to keep being loved. I still have to remind myself of that with my kids. This is a generational thing, which started with Meme, my Mom, and then me. Part of healing is knowing. Knowing gives you the power to make a change.

Now, my Meme was amazing; she kept our family super tight. As she got older, she had many health problems. Her back issues were from years of moving furniture to clean, cooking all day, and not asking for help. She wore her sweet body out. From her mid-70s until she died at 83, she always had major back pain and arthritis. I wish I could have helped her more toward the end, but I was on my own journey living in California.

I'll never forget the day I got the call that she was gone. She had been put into hospice. I had a dream the night she died that she said, "Polly, I didn't mean to go to sleep and stay asleep." I woke up the following day to the call. My Meme had gone to be with Jesus. She was in the hospital because she had many stomach problems. The place gave her morphine for pain; her body couldn't handle it, and her heart stopped.

My Mom and I were the only kids that left Arkansas at that point. So we flew with both my kids to Arkansas for the funeral. I just kept thinking and remembering my whole life. I went back and forth there, so England always felt like going home. The morning of the funeral, I had such a weird feeling that I had to go to the funeral home before the funeral home opened.

 It was about 6 am. The night before viewing the body, my little Carmen was about seven. She had a mood ring on her finger. She was the last one with me to see the body before they closed the casket. Carmen took her ring off and put the ring next to Memes' arm, tucked deep in the casket, and said, "I'll always be with you, Meme." The funeral home owners closed the casket right after.

The next morning, I called one of my friends in town that I grew up with. I said, "You have to come get me. I have to go to the funeral home now."

So she came in her pajamas right then. That's the beautiful thing about the South: those friends will be there for you when you need them, even if they're mad at you.

So we drove to the funeral home. I had the owners open the home just for me. I must have looked like a crazy person in pajamas, with no make-up, bedhead twilight. In a small town, they get it. So she opened the room where the casket was and turned the lights on. Then she opened the casket because I just had to see Meme one time alone. There on her chest by her heart was that little ring.

No one saw that Carmen put it there, and the casket was closed right after we all left the night before. I believed that Meme came down from heaven and moved it there to show me she was at peace, and we would always be in her heart, even in heaven.

So we drove home frantically because I wanted to get home before the kids got up, and we had to prepare for the funeral. My Mom was awake before I told her what had just happened. She said, "Polly, I had the weirdest dream about Meme last night."

I was on pins and needles because I wanted to know I wasn't losing my mind, and I saw what I saw. She said, "In my dream, Meme got the little ring Carmen put by her side, and she moved it to her heart." I started bawling, and I told her what had just happened. It was total confirmation.

She was selfless; even in death, she wanted everyone to be happy. I wish she were here to read this book so she would know how much everyone loved her. My Grandpa is the only man in my entire life I trusted 100%, and I knew he really loved and accepted me. When my Dad was gone, Papa stepped up to be like a Father figure. In my eyes, he did no wrong. That was way different than some of my family's experiences of him.

Papa was born in Arkansas, and his Mom died when he was eleven. His Dad built roads all over Arkansas and Alabama. Papa was the baby and moved from tent to tent as a boy with his older sister and Dad. He married my Grandmother when he was twenty-six years old, and she was sixteen. Papa worked as a farmer for years. He also was in the navy for a few years and would write beautiful love letters to my Meme while he was gone. He opened the Dairy Delight in England, Arkansas, when he was around fifty. Papa was thick-headed and a man of few words, and he loved the weather channel and Fox News.

When I lived in Memphis from five to sixteen years old, his Meme would visit us. We lived in a cute little neighborhood in Fox Meadows. This was a suburb back in the day in Memphis. Now it's a super ghetto place. Back then, it had a fantastic pool and clubhouse. Some of my best memories growing up were when they visited. My Papa and I would go to the pool and swim. Even in his 70s, I remember he would dive off the diving board.

When he went home, it was back to work. He worked every day till the last four years of his life. He was around ninety-three when he stopped going to the Dairy Delight. He drove one block until one day, he hit a trash can and thought it was a kid. Then he realized he was almost blind and didn't drive anymore. He was super tight with money and didn't want Meme to spend money on things, which caused a lot of tension between them. His growing up so poor and with one parent made him afraid of not having any money.

One of my sweetest memories was when he took me to the London house in England. Back then, England had a thriving main street with many cute boutiques. He asked me to pick out something. He picked it out because I wanted to spend only a little. It was a corduroy dress that I had worn for years. I remember putting it on and feeling guilty that I got something special that he picked out and no one else did. I downplayed that dress and wouldn't wear it in England to not upset anyone. There was much jealousy among some of my cousins because he showed favoritism to me.

I think he felt sorry for me. I would downplay how close we were to avoid confrontation or for anyone to talk about me.

I learned at an early age to be a people pleaser. Looking back, it wasn't my fault I was closer to him than many people. I was a very loving, sweet kid and always told him how cool he was and how much I loved him as a kid. If you're a favorite, you often feel guilty. So if that's you, realize you just had a stronger connection to that person, and it's ok.

Papa lived a few years longer than my Meme. When he went to the nursing home, he regretted not appreciating how great my Meme was and how hard she worked. He didn't ever tell her how great she was or how much he appreciated her till it was too late. That's why we have to tell people how we feel so we don't have any regrets. Papa died at ninety-eight and was buried in England in that plot I partied on when I was fourteen, right next to Meme. I came from solid stock with some hardship but excellent hard, working, God-fearing, good folks. It's incredible how one bad apple can spoil the whole barrel. Thus my Dad...

Chapter 4

JUST ME AND ESTHER JEAN: HISTORY REPEATS ITSELF PART 2

Some great advice I was given long ago is remembering where you came from. Remember the pain you were rescued from but don't let it define you. Let it liberate you to free others. If the Creator of the world can create us out of the dust, imagine what you can do out of all the experiences you've had on earth, we can be pitiful or powerful; the choice is yours. Sit on your pity pot and complain or arise as my Momma did. She still does every day at 77 years old.

As I told you earlier, I wrote a story at Orange Coast Community College during my freshman year called "Guilt, Sex, and My Little Child." I will rewrite this paper in this chapter from a broader perspective.

After her divorce from my Dad, my Mom immersed herself in work. She was a workaholic or an overachiever. Usually, when we push so hard at something in our life, it's because we are shoving down something else, or there would be balance. She worked all the time. I remember she had a pager when I was around seven years old. If you're a millennial, you are like- A what?

You wore a pager on your waist or shoved in your purse. It was a device that would beep when someone needed you to call them. It would beep with a number on it. Then you would go to the nearest pay phone or any phone and call the number back. See, we didn't have cell phones to call you. So one night, she had it with her, and the pager went off. It literally went off all day and night.

Mom helped start Federal Express. All of their planes were loaded at night from the shipping warehouse and departed at about midnight so packages could be delivered in 24 hours. My Mom sometimes gets calls saying, "We left a load at one of the warehouses, and it has to go on this last outgoing flight. Can you go get it?" So she would load me up at midnight and drive down to the warehouse to pick up the package and take it to the plane.

She was wholly committed to helping this company be a success. So this night in particular, she was over it. I remember her putting it in the toilet. She was so happy because she felt free. Trust me, she got another one within a day but had a moment of liberation. Now let me return to my grandparents to set up for Esther Jean in time. That's where a lot of the dysfunction began. I call it a generational curse. My Grandpa was one of two boys and one girl. His Mom died early, and the kids had to be raised by the Dad. He became an overworker and didn't pay much attention to the kids.

The one sister fell victim to abuse. She was the only girl in an isolated situation, so he took his frustration out on her. There is never an excuse for abuse of any kind, EVER! I'm just stating his mindset. My Papa didn't know anything about this. This was the beginning of my Papa not being connected emotionally. So he married my Meme, who was neglected as a child and had her own issues. She was non-emotional and dealt with her pain by cleaning and cooking. So her eyes were blinded to what was happening beneath her very eyes. We work out our past sometimes in ways that we are unconscious of that can unknowingly affect our kids.

My grandparents had four kids in the middle of nowhere. They lived on a farm with a neighbor they said was a dirty old man. He was my Moms first abuser when she was four. When she told my Grandparents, my Meme took him out in the yard, and they were going to beat him. My Mom said he fell to the ground and started acting crazy. They told him to get out of there and never come back. So he did. As a young girl, this tormented my Mom because she never got to tell how she felt or felt safe anymore. This left her open to more abuse. See, sexual predators look for the easy prey, which is extra sick.

Papa, at the beginning of their marriage, was an alcoholic and would come home and take his frustration out on the kids at home and cousins, that would stay and work on the farm. One, in particular, was picked on the most. So he would take out his frustration on the youngest girl. This was the other perpetrator of sexual abuse from males in her life. That youngest girl was my Mom. She, even then, was so giving. She said he didn't hurt her. She knew it was wrong, but she also felt sorry for him. He was picked on by Papa a lot, and so she felt sorry for him. This continued until one day, her sister found out and told her she was a dirty little girl. This is where the shame and guilt began for her.

After her cousin did this, it started with her Grandpa, my Papa's Dad. He would show up at the farm, bring goodies just for Mom, and ask Meme if he could ride Momma. Meme was dealing with her own torment inside and didn't even get that that was going on with her baby girl, so she would let her go. When Mom went into therapy, she remembered she was molested from when she was three until eleven.

The Grandpa never remarried, so he preyed on an innocent young girl because he knew he could. He also could feel like a man because he was impotent, and a little girl wouldn't know the difference. How sick, but this is how predators work: they find the sweet ones. This is how the devil works: he is a slippery snake that finds who he can devour and tries to ruin their calling and life.

All this locked my Mom's mind into feeling like something was wrong with her and that she didn't deserve real love and trust. She never told my

Grandma. My Meme just knew about the first one. By this time, my Mom was too ashamed to tell anyone that it happened again. My Mom knew she was busy cooking for the family and running the house, so she never told her again until she was forty. Your voice matters, so please find someone to tell if this has happened or is happening to you. YOU MATTER!

It's strange how history repeats itself, even if you hate what happened to you. That's why I'm writing this, so you will do an inventory of the events that have happened to you in your life. Hit pause, get some counseling, and don't make the same mistakes because of ignorance. Ignorance is not stupidity.

It just means you have a blind spot. We are victims of most evil that happens to us as children. This can define us unless we properly file these actions and get it's not our fault and nothing is wrong with us. We are innocent children in a situation that we did not create nor deserve,

When I wrote that paper at OCC, it was four weeks after my eyes were opened. A man named Don came to my human sexuality class with Dr. Mona Coates. He started telling the story of his growing up and what happened. He said he would be taken in the barn when he was a boy and transported himself on the beams of light out of there when he was abused. His family members would molest him there for years. He learned to disassociate at that moment and not be able to feel. He had many failed relationships until he healed that inner child of his.

His mission in life became to tell his story to give freedom to us still in darkness. I believe God sent him to help me become free of my shame. God is a God of order and perfect timing. I couldn't have handled this while still living in Memphis. Being in California, I felt much more peace and freedom in talking about my past. That's why the teacher showed up. The teacher appears when the student is ready.

When he started telling the story, I broke down like I had never cried. After class, I approached him in my long white hippie skirt and no shoes and dreads and told him how brave he was. He noticed when I talked to him that I couldn't stop blinking. He asked me a little about my childhood. At that point, I had no memories of anything except what I knew about my Dad and all that drama. He asked me if I would like to have a free counseling session with him at his office. I had never had any counseling, and I was nineteen, so I thought that was pretty cool. I remember going home and telling my Mom this story of Don. She was so touched and told me it was good for me to go. She had just started seeing a counselor and was starting to remember her past.

My Mom grew up on that farm with all those awful things that happened to her and never told anyone. She held all that guilt and shame inside, just did her chores, and was grateful she had a home. When she moved to England at thirteen, she went to work and had a lot of friends in high school. She was a good girl and only had one boyfriend in high school, and she dated him till he went away to war. Then she married my Dad, got divorced, and had me all alone. We either internalize or externalize when we don't work out whatever happened to us as a child. My Mom did both.

It's always been Esther Jean and me from the Dairy Queen. I went that day to Don's office. I remember getting there and parking my gold 87 Jeep Wrangler with tons of hippie stickers all over it in the parking lot.

Here she is, the golden girl that drove me to almost 50 states in 3 years This was my baby. She had traveled over 60,000 miles in a year and a half following the Grateful Dead

I was so nervous walking into his office that I had no idea what to expect. As I walked into his office, I could feel my throat close. I felt gripping fear and anxiety about what was going to happen. He sat me down and asked why his story touched me so deeply. I had no idea.

My Mom and I had just moved to California via New York. So I had been gone from my Arkansas family for almost 2 years. It may have touched me because he was from the South, too, and his story was so sad. I told him the story about my Dad, and we did a session on that. After seeing me a few times, he finally said, "Polly, you didn't cry and got so triggered by my story because you're sad about your Dad. You cried because it probably happened to you." I left that day in shock, trying to remember if that had happened to me.

I drove back to our cool condo at the top of the cliffs in Newport Beach from Irvine. I remember kissing my cousin at my grandmas at seven. That wasn't it. I remember being inappropriate with boys when I was at home, and my Mom was at work from twelve to fourteen. None of those memories struck a deep chord.

I went home and asked my Mom if anything I didn't remember had happened to me. She was in her therapy and told me about what happened to her. Then I knew I needed to dig deeper to see if I had any memories. My Mom's story made me see her with fresh eyes. I knew then why she worked so hard when I was young and strived to get ahead.

She worked sixty to seventy hours a week. She did this to give me the best and worked out all her pain from growing up. Yes, my Mom used everything that happened to her for good, but she was in inner turmoil. After she told me her story, she told me she thought I should do more counseling. That night I met with Don, walked on the beach, and talked about everything. He said, "I want you to see my therapist Gloria. She is so helpful and does some cool exercises to unlock memories." So I said, "Ok," I trusted Don. He was the first guy that didn't try to hit on me in any way, so I felt safe."

The next day I made my appointment with Gloria. I told her the story about Don, what he had shared, and how it affected me. So she asked me to trust her. She had beautiful red hair and brown eyes like my Mom. The teacher appears when the student is ready. I felt an immediate connection with her and knew I was safe.

When I walked into her office that day, she had me sit comfortably on the sofa, breathe deeply, and close my eyes. She walked me through an exercise where she would ask about my childhood and go through different body parts to see if I felt anything. I didn't feel anything till I got to my throat. She said, "Describe the feeling in your throat?" I said, "I feel like I'm choking." She asked, "What's the first time you felt that?"

That's when I returned to the memory I had locked inside all these years. My Mom barely dated growing up because she was so busy and didn't want what happened to her to happen to me. She dated this one guy for about six months or so named Charlie.

When I went back in my memory, I remember being terrified of him. Then I remembered what he would do. He would ask my sweet single Mom if he could help and tuck me in. He then would take me upstairs to my room and molest me and grab my throat. He would tell me he would do that to my Mom if I ever told anyone, and I would have to live with him. He would choke me to the point that I had better not say a thing or make a sound so my Mom could live. Guess my age; yep, you guessed it, I was four. History repeated itself. So, of course, my throat is where I had all my locked memories. We store trauma in different places in our bodies.

Many men and women go to battle and come back with PTSD and store their pain in their bodies. I know one man that would get terrible migraines. When he finally allowed himself to talk about what he witnessed, he began to have fewer migraines. When you are traumatized as a child, it is as if you were in a war, and your body processes that trauma differently. I held all my memories in my throat.

As a four-year-old, I didn't realize he wouldn't kill my Mom. The only person I had was my Mom. My grandparents were over 2 hours away. My Dad wasn't really in the picture, so I believed him. Every night he would ask if he could tuck me in, and then that would happen. I don't remember how far it went. I remember staring at my clown picture in my room when it would happen. I am finally not afraid of clowns to this day, but it took much counseling and praying to get over it. After they broke up, I never slept in my own bed till I was a teen. I started wetting the bed again, and my Mom couldn't figure out why. I would also sit in my closet in my room in the dark. One night my Mom listened outside the door to hear what I was doing. I would sit in there and say, "damn, hell, damn, hell, and other curse words" repeatedly. One time I packed my little suitcase, came downstairs out of nowhere, and told my Mom I was running away.

My Mom was my best friend, and I wanted to leave. These were all signs that I was in turmoil early in life. At this point, my Mom had not done her own therapy, so she had no idea what was happening, nor could she even imagine something so horrific. I still sleep with a night light to this day.

The enemy comes like a thief in the night to steal, kill, and destroy. If this resonates with you, please, I beg you, please talk to someone. Find a safe space to tell this treachery. Ask God to heal your pain. Please know that you never did anything to deserve being abused. My prayer is that my story brings deliverance and freedom to you.

Finally, to be free and file that memory where it belongs in the past with no shame or guilt. You are free of this; it's not your fault. I'm so sorry this happened to you. I am free now of all the pain that terrible event in my life caused and how much havoc it did. I want you to be free too. I never told my Mom till that day with Gloria. I woke up from unlocking that memory with Gloria. I was on the floor hysterically crying and shaking in a fetal position. She was petting my hair, saying it's ok, he's gone. He can never hurt you again. I literally went back to that time and felt I was there. This is what had to happen so I could heal that little girl. She told me to go home and rest, and I literally relived what had happened. I drove home like something had been undone and slept for a full day. I did exactly what I did when that pastor came to my house to tell me my Daddy had killed himself. I detached from my feelings, and I felt the same. See, when we have trauma, we fight or flee. Your brain cannot distinguish between reality and memory. This is why it's so important to have tools to process these things and correctly place them so they don't rear their ugly head later in life.

My Mom would have never put me in harm's way. She had no idea that she was attracted to what she knew. Our unconscious mind is powerful if we let it stay unconscious. We will draw situations to ourselves or our kids that repeat our past, not purposefully. It's called a generational curse.

Today I know all my generational curses are broken. Jesus didn't just come for the perfect. He came to hold us from all our pain because we live in a fallen world. He came to set us all free. After much work and prayer, I can see where curses are in my life now and go to the root and get them out so no future generation needs to suffer. After I had this memory, I did a few sessions with Gloria, but I didn't completely heal my soul. My go-to was to run. I became an expert marathon runner, and I did for years. Not having a Dad who protected or loved me affected many of my decisions, even though I had a wonderful Mom and family. I would have told him if I knew I had a Dad that could protect me. Now I know I've always had a Dad that loved me, my Heavenly Father.

If you're wondering what happened to Charlie, it's pretty fitting. After I told my Mom when I was nineteen, we went to Arkansas shortly after. My family had a tradition of going to horse races in Hot Springs every year. This time my Mom saw Charlie; she was shocked she hadn't seen him since they broke up when I was four. He was on an oxygen tank, looked like death warmed over, and was in a wheelchair because he was paralyzed.

My Mom said her first instinct was to push his wheelchair down the stairs. Then she realized that would be the easy way out for him. That he would endure suffering the way he was for way longer. Karma Always Pays Back! I forgave Charlie because I can only imagine what sick things happened to him for him to do what he did to a four-year-old. Once I had that revelation, I let it go.

Chapter 5

RUNNING

Like I said, after Charlie, my Mom never really dated anymore. We lived in Memphis, and I went to a very conservative Baptist Christian School my entire educational years. All through elementary school, I was a fun kid. My entire world depended on if my friends liked me. My Mom would come into my room, and Adeline and I would be on the telephone. Yes, a landline for hours talking.

Our neighborhood was about 10 minutes from my elementary school. It was a modest neighborhood with 80 townhomes. They were like a duplex, but each half was different on the outside. Each home was painted different colors so you could differentiate the homes from each other. As a kid, I thought they were so beautiful. My Mom got a loan from my Papa for $5000 for the down payment. The last dollar she got from my Dad was when he pulled up in his jet and gave her a measly $2000.

She signed the agreement for that house on the premise that he would give her all the back child support. He owed for about two years. Of course, he didn't come through, and she asked her Dad. I come from good stock! My Mom paid my Papa back $200 a month until she paid back every penny. Yes, we ate a lot of Wendy's, but I only went with, and my Mom kept her word, which was terrific, but her parents were people of their word.

The house was upstairs and downstairs and was $40,000 in 1976. It was on the corner, within walking distance of the clubhouse and pool. That is where I spent most of my summers, and almost all my birthdays were in the clubhouse. I had my own room with a giant closet and window seats that my Mom had custom pillows made for. I thought it was the most beautiful house ever. When I dream, I dream of that house.

In the '70s, not many women were raising their kids alone. Remember, all my growing-up years, I thought my Dad was dead. I thought that until he arose like Lazareth when I was almost 16. I also was carrying those deep secrets of being violated as a child. I believe my abandonment issues didn't make me run as a child; it was more of the shame from the abuse at age four. I knew as a kid that my Dad had some love for me, but I always felt second because he picked his new family over me. That is the script I wrote in my head. Then when he rose from the dead, and I found out that they got to spend some time with him while he was a fugitive, I knew it was true. I wasn't as important as them.

I made that mean something about my own self-worth. I had not realized that I had been plucked out of a corrupt system by God's grace. My school was mainly upper-class kids with two parents. I didn't feel ashamed of my Mom being single because I could say as a kid my Dad was dead. My Mom trusted me and let me go home after school alone at around thirteen. This was when my shame started to show, and I started acting out, and my mask went up. When I would go to school, I would follow the rules, and on Sunday, I would go to Sunday school, but I always felt different. My rebellious spirit made me feel like I was always off. I didn't know why I acted out. I would hang out with the neighborhood kids when I came home from school. They all went to the school around the corner, which was a public school. No one but one friend went to my school; just the public school wild kids were in my hood.

When I would come home from school, I would go where my Mom asked me not to. I would go to the ditch around the corner. It was a little stream in a canyon in the woods. That's where I would meet all Wooddale kids, smoke pot, and ride BMX. I still have a sheet of paper from 82 and 83 that named all the boys I made out with and the dates. I never had sex with anyone, but I did things I was so ashamed of and didn't want my Christian school friends to know. I would have been so done if I would have had social media back then!

On Friday nights, my Mom would take me to the local skating rink. I told her they locked us in, and we couldn't get out. I was #2 in the state for speed skating, so she thought I was telling the truth. I would skate for a few hours, then sneak out with a friend to drink or go to the skate park next door. The first time I remember getting so drunk, I got alcohol poisoning at thirteen.

I had a friend who was a few years older than me, and she went to another public school. I wanted her to like me so bad that I went with her to do whatever. This particular Friday night at the east end of the skating rink, she had two eighteen-year-old boys pick us up. They came in their new Camaro to pick us up. I knew it was wrong, but I wanted to be cool and protect her.

I sat up front, and she got in the back with one of the guys. When we pulled up to the liquor store, the driver asked me what I wanted to drink. At this point, I had only had a Pina Colada or a Margarita, or a beer I stole from the fridge. I saw a big picture of a bottle of Jack Daniels on the wall. I said I wanted that. He looked at me and asked, "Are you sure?" Of course, I answered very coyly, "Yeah, get me the big bottle."

We drove around, and I drank almost the entire bottle alone. I was sitting the whole time, so the alcohol hadn't gone to my head yet.

I looked in the backseat, and my friend was almost naked and about to have sex with the guy. I said what are you doing to her? "The guy answered, "Your friend is a slut, and she wants to do this!" I told the driver I was sick and told him to take us back now, or I would call the police for rape. I had no idea if that would work. The driver said I'll take you back now and told my friend to put on her clothes. When we returned to the skating rink's east end, my friend was so mad at me.

Suddenly, I started vomiting all over the parking lot. I had to get my stomach pumped that night. When my Mom picked me up, I was just out of it. I didn't tell her the truth until much later, and my supposed friend never talked to me again. God protected me, but why was I in so much pain that I got hammered? I did not know how to fix my eyes on God, and He would carry my burden. I didn't even remember my pain yet.

My Dad did not come back to life yet, so I didn't have all the super Daddy issues yet. I also had not had all the memories resurface about what happened with Charlie when I was four years old, so I was pushing the pain down. That girl never hung out with me again, but it's OK. Sometimes you are being protected, and you think it's rejection. That same girl grew up and had four different baby daddies and several abortions. I'm sure she had some unresolved pain that manifested in destroying her life.

I remember another time I went to a party that was around the corner from my house while my Mom was at work. There were kids smoking pot, and they had a huge tree house in the backyard where people were drinking. We must've been thirteen or fourteen years old. In the middle of the party, granted, it was like 1 p.m. in the summer; this stupid kid pulled out a knife and thought it was cool. Dumb me, the protector, grabbed him to make him stop swaying the knife around. However, when I went to grab it, he accidentally stabbed me in the arm. I was bleeding everywhere, and I guess that was an excellent way to stop the party, so it was over. I went home and cleaned up my wound and never told my Mom.

When I was almost fourteen, my Mom got an awful phone call from Child Protective Services. Somebody had reported to them that my Mom was allowing drinking in her house, allowing underage girls to have sex and that I was even stabbed in the process. The CPS worker said they would take my Mom away from me and that I would have to go into foster care.

That triggered something so intense I felt pain in my throat. Anxiety makes you feel like you can't breathe. I was gasping for air and trying to get the words out to the lady about what I had been doing behind my Mom's back. That was exactly what Charlie said to me when I was four. I was reliving what had happened, and I felt my biggest fear was about to come true, losing my Mom. I could not remember all the Sunday school lessons I learned about Jesus calming the storm and telling the wind peace to be still. I had no clue how to calm myself. That day I had a shift in my soul. Every single bit of church I had been practicing came to my heart, and I told my Mom everything. I told the CPS lady everything.

The woman was African American and about 35 years old. I could feel her relief when I was honest. She told me how lucky I was that she took my word on it because she would have taken me away from my Mom. The warning was set that day like a line in the sand. She said there were not any more phone calls. My Mom was devastated. Her entire life had been about me, and I felt like I failed her again. I didn't know why I behaved like that or why I would jeopardize losing my Mom.

When we leave things inside the drawer, they become moldy. If you know what I mean, I didn't know what I didn't know. It was a blind spot in my past that had me continue to do things to sabotage my life. So I could get what I thought I deserved. REJECTION!

I shaped up that day, and I stopped hanging out with all the friends in my neighborhood. I stopped riding BMX with all those kids. I stopped going to my neighbor's house, borrowing his little motorcycle, doing wheelies in the neighborhood, and stealing all his mini liquor bottles. I attended my Christian school and joined a high school sorority called Chi Sigma Omega. I started hanging out with all the kids at school that weren't so destructive. Even my best friend was a pastor's kid, and my other best friend was one of the daughters of the largest car dealers in Memphis. I had lots of new preppy friends too. We would have parties, go to their farmhouses, and have keggers like normal high school stuff. I even became the very best pledge, which was crazy. When I came home one day, I remembered that they had decorated my room with the most beautiful balloons and decorations so I would join their sorority.

I was honored. I was so glad they didn't know how wild I was before this. This is part of the mask that went up even taller. A mask of shame and guilt. If we are children of our Heavenly Father, then we know that He took all of that guilt and shame and nailed it to the cross. I didn't get that at all! I was deep in my shame!

Then right after I became the best pledge at the end of my 10th grade year when I was almost sixteen, I saw the ad in the paper that said my Dad was alive. Holy Crap! This was around the same time my Mom met this man in California. It was all happening at once.

See, my Mom barely dated while I was growing up. She had a couple of boyfriends, but she was really just with me. It was just me and Esther Jean. I think somewhere inside her, she was scared that something could happen to me as it did her. Little did she know it had already happened.

On one business trip, I remember when she came home, she was different. I was almost sixteen and stayed with our sweet neighbors around the corner, Patsy and Pert. They would babysit me when my Mom had to go out of town to Memphis for business.

This time was way different when my Mom walked in. She had a special glow on her face. She met someone, and his name was Guy. She fell madly in love with him. This was probably her first time being intimate with a man in 10 years. I would have fallen in love with anybody at that point too.

I went away that summer to Vacation Bible school at the beach. I had an encounter with the Holy Spirit that I had never felt before. My teeth chattered, and I was shaking on the beach. I could feel something move into my body. It was the power of the Holy Spirit, and I've only felt that a couple of times in my whole life. When I came home on the bus, I looked out the window, and my Mom was standing there.

Now my Mom was kind of an overweight lady my whole life, but today, she looks like she has lost 20 pounds. I had only been gone a couple of weeks. During that time, she got to see Guy again and fell deeper in love. She was dressed sexy, which she didn't usually do. My red flags went up big time. We went out to eat at Red Lobster. That was our go-to "special "place. I looked at her hands and thought how skinnier her hands were. She told me she would do everything she could to be with him and that she was utterly in love.

I remember judging everything that came out of her mouth. I remember what I was eating. I was eating clam chowder, and I was just so angry inside. I'm sure I felt like I would be abandoned by her, too, and what would I have to hold onto? All the church camp stuff went right out the window. I didn't even allow God to go deep enough to fill me with His peace.

Within a few months, Gary reappeared and rose from the dead. I did what I used to do. I got another set of friends besides the "good kids." They were the edgy punkers. All these life events put me on a path of wanting to run and run hard. It's when the real mask went up.

I want you to do a little exercise. I call it the "Authenticity unmasking" event.

Please look inside yourself and see which of these masks you recognize from your wardrobe or life. Please use this time to pick a couple and describe a recent typical time when you've worn one of these masks.

1. I'm a happy mask
2. I'm better than most mask
3. I'm very together mask

4. I'm a victim of others mask
5. I don't care about mask
6. I am a self-sufficient mask
7. I'm a very important mask
8. I'm confident enough not to need a love mask
9. I'm the expert mask and the theologically trained professional mask
10. I'm not hurt mask
11. I have the answers mask
12. I am an independent mask
13. I am a cool mask

Sometimes we wear a mask to please others; sometimes, there's just so much pain we want to hide our painful junk from the world so that the image they see won't be shattered. Now ask yourself this question.

What reaction do you fear if you remove the mask and reveal the real you?

I found out that I would be a leader. I discovered I wore the mask because I feared not being enough or people would judge me. That people would think I'm too crazy and that I'm not pure enough to be an excellent Godly example because I'm still not perfect. We are constantly under construction, but having all the necessary pieces for the project sure helps get the road to inner joy and peace together more smoothly!

When we found out my Dad was alive, we lived in Memphis. Of course, my Mom said, "I'll take you to see him." She drove down to Jacksonville, which is where he was. Now remember, my entire life, I thought he was dead, and now all of a sudden, he's alive. I walked into the room where they had him. He was handcuffed behind his back, and his feet were cuffed together like an animal. I had not seen him since I was a kid and had no idea he was alive.

The room was round. It was the attorney's room where we met. There were books all on the wall. The two jailers who brought him in treated him like El Chapo. They were almost respectful to him. I looked at the police officer and said, "My Dad is not an animal. You must let him go right now so he can hug me." I can't even believe I talked to an officer like that at almost sixteen years old. So they let him go, and I was able to hug him. I just collapsed in his arms.

That's when shame came up, and another shift happened inside my soul. I did not let anyone at school know what was happening except for my best friend, who had known me since elementary school. I felt ashamed and embarrassed because all those rich kids had no craziness in their life as I did. That's when I started hanging out more with the punk rockers. Even back then, I could tell who would judge me more harshly and who wouldn't. Those kids had been through a lot, so I felt safe with them. You would generally feel safe with the rich, "normal" kids.

There was this one girl that had a Mohawk and drove a cool convertible Mustang. I felt safe with those kids and knew that if they knew about my Dad, they wouldn't judge me or look down on me. On the weekends, she would take me to the 'Antenna,' a punk rock club.

I would pack Knox gelatin in my bag to make my hair a Mohawk. I would put on ripped jeans or Levi's and put a chain around my belt holes with a lock.

I wore black combat boots, a long John shirt, and a flannel; this was a standard uniform for punk rock chicks in the 80s. We went and saw some fantastic punk bands. I still had my preppy friends and did the sorority thing, but I also had this other side.

That became a pattern for thirty-five years, having my feet in two worlds, and I am still working on it. Those kids were edgier. Inside I had nothing but edges, so it felt safe.

I remember once we went and saw two bands, 'The Exploited' and a band called 'The UK Subs.' They were pretty cool punk bands. I was hanging out backstage, and the bassist with the most incredible fire engine, a red Mohawk, asked me if I wanted to go on tour. I felt like that four-year-old that packed her suitcase and wanted to run away from home again. I thought deeply and hard about it and was ready to run.

Then like an angel, the lead singer of one of the bands asked me, "How old are you?" I told him how old I was, and he said I will protect you from yourself; you don't need to be here. You have somebody in your life that loves you. I can tell by your heart, and I will ask you not to be backstage because things will happen back here that I don't want you to be a part of. Even back then, God used a punk rocker to protect me from me. I stopped hanging out with those kids, and that's when my Mom got the opportunity to move to New York.

I want you to pause and think of all the times when things could have gone way worse. You had angels protecting you, just like I did in that cold dark Smokey backstage at that punk club. About three months later, I found out I had a sister I had never known about. She is eight years older than me. All this happened before the Internet and cell phones. After my parent's divorce, my mother wanted little to do with anything that had to do with Gary. She knew about my big sister, but she also knew that her Mom was mistreated by Dad too.

When Dad "died," I think that both of our moms kept us apart, not because of their being mean but out of the pain they both had because of what my Dad put them through. I instantly loved my big sister, so that was a blessing. My Dad had remarried a woman that was this cool Hippie lady that had no idea that my Dad was a drug dealer, and he had four other kids. He was under the alias of Lucas

Harmony. They had a child together under 1 when Dad got busted. The day I met my sister, we were all in North Carolina, where he had been moved after he had been arrested in Florida. That was an awesome day.

We all united in North Carolina, all of what I call now his **original kids**. All these things immediately put my brain on a frequency to run, fight, or flight. I chose flight. As a kid, I did the same thing, and now I had more things on top of more things to deal with, even though I hadn't even dealt with my past yet.

In my junior year in high school, my Mom got an opportunity to leave Federal Express. My Mom helped build this company, and many people were jealous of her position in the company and made up lies about her. They were trying to steal her job and make it look like all the stories they made up to make her look bad were all true. My Mom had dedicated her entire corporate life to building this company. Her best friend was the mother of the man that started the company. He had his hands tied because he couldn't show favoritism to her, but everything that was going on was a lie.

Mom told me, "I'm going to resign from Federal Express, and we're going to move to New York." This was my senior year in high school. I had spent my entire life going to school with my same friends. All of these events happened all at once. I was ready to run again within about a year and a half. I did not want to be there anymore. I figured if I just kept moving, all my pain wouldn't follow.

I was so confused the day we packed up, left everybody behind, and moved to New York. I was an angry little girl and took my frustrations out on her many times on the way, even though I said it was a great idea. I just was confused inside myself. Living in New York was wild. I was a little southern girl, and I didn't know anything. I already told you my crazy story about the fire drill, but that's just one of many.

I wanted to model, so I got skinny enough to start modeling gigs. This is when I learned all about bulimia. I just knew I could eat what I wanted and puke and be skinny. This affected me for a long time. Always thinking I was fat even when I wasn't. How you feel about your Dad and how you think he feels about you is directly related to your self-image. That's why it's so important to know that you are perfectly created and loved by another Father who will never let you down. I did a few little gigs in New York. On the weekends, my friends and I would take the train to the city and go to nightclubs with our fake IDs.

It was the first time I felt like an adult, and I was party Polly. I remember my Mom had someone follow me at school. She had a threat that I was going to be kidnapped. I never knew till recently. This was because my Dad was on trial. He was telling on our government about the whole

Iran Contra scandal in the 80s, and the cartel thought he would rat them out. So, now I know many people wanted to kidnap me. My Mom had a bodyguard follow me around at school, and my Mom was on pins and needles to get us to Cali, partially out of fear because of Dad but also because that is where Guy was (her love). We spent about a year and a half in New York.

Esther Jean would take me down to Memphis to see my Dad in prison, and we would do that at least three times a year while I lived in New York. She also did it so that I could see my friends. Friends were the most important thing to me. I didn't realize it, but getting crumbs from my father in prison took a more profound toll on my self-worth. It was cool listening to him putting the pieces together of what had happened his whole life. I was so impressed by his gangster life, like he was a superhero to me back then. I had not yet put all the pieces together of how he treated my mother because she never told me.

After graduating from High School, we moved to California, where the wild journey began. I call that my Hippie years and my "Uncracking the mask box" years.

Chapter 6

CALIFORNIA: THE HIPPIE DAYS' ROUND 1

This is where my healing journey began as you read in chapter four. Sorry, I skipped around a little bit. "California prophet on a burning shore" was a lyric from one of my favorite songs, "Estimated Prophet" from The Grateful Dead. I call these my hippy days because, during this time, I saw over 200 Grateful Dead shows and went on to see another 150 once I moved back to Atlanta.

Esther and I are on the road again. It was time to set our sails and move west because her job in New York was over. Her long-awaited reunification with her man Guy was about to happen. Guy was the one she was so skinny from hanging out with while I was at church camp when I was sixteen. Jealousy was there, and I wasn't looking forward to meeting him.

When we got to California, we moved into the Marriott. It was amazing. It had a swim-up bar pool, Jacuzzi, and a killer workout room and sat in the highest-end shopping center in the country. Mom was at work every day because she drove to Los Angeles from Newport Beach to work. After all, she didn't want to live in LA. Her job was up there, so she did the 1-2 hour commute daily. She is a woman of no compromise. She knew she wanted to live in Newport Beach and only came to California to settle.

I had just graduated from high school, and I felt so free. I knew no one out there, so I could run hard, and no one would even know that's what I was doing. I knew I loved the beach, so I would go to this fantastic peninsula called Balboa every day. It was part of Newport Beach. It is about 3 miles long and less than a mile wide. This was the first time I had seen something like it. People rode skateboards on the boardwalk next to the ocean with surfboards on their bikes and girls skating in their bikinis. It was so Cali!

One day I was sitting at Balboa Pier and watching the skim borders that would go on all day. One of them finally came over to talk to me. I'll call him skimboarding Steve. He had beautiful brown hair, tan skin, chapped lips from surfing every day, and that funny surf Brah accent. He thought I was the cat's meow, so we started dating, and he introduced me to his family. I immediately felt a connection. We even carved our name in a tree still there in Newport Beach 30 years later. That relationship ended, but we are still in contact all these years later. He watched me go from this cute southern girl to this wild hippie chic.

My mask began to appear again even bigger in California with more masks on top of more layers. The man we went to California to be with completely disappeared after the first six months. I'm sure my Mom was devastated. I was too busy with new adventures to really know what was up. She put on the mask, so it didn't bother me. I'm a professional and work hard, and I don't have to face this pain mask. She hadn't even dealt with her stuff from growing up or my Dad yet.

After about three months at the hotel, we finally moved to a cool townhome, and I started making friends slowly. My neighbors were skateboarders. Every night eight guys and two girls, me and another chic, would meet at the top of what we called Suicide Hill. The goal was to skate through the speed wobbles and make it down the mountain without eating it. I was a bit of a tomboy, so falling didn't scare me. I ate it many times, and my knees looked like road rash.

I started learning to surf, and I still wanted to model some. I enrolled in an acting school that was part of Lee Strasburg. My acting coach believed in me, but he knew I had much growing up to do. If you ever read this, you're the best, RJ Adams from the Actors Workshop in Laguna Niguel. Right after we got to Cali, I got my golden girl Jeep. The beautiful Jeep in the pictures earlier that I pulled up to that wonderful therapist in. I lived with a surfboard attached to the roof.

I had an agent in LA and was starting to get minor acting roles. One day it was our showcase for acting when all the big shots from LA came down. I pulled up with wet hair from the beach, no shoes, and I was 30 minutes late. This became part of my mask to fulfill the prophecy I felt I deserved. The mask of I'm not good enough, and I'm A FAILURE; YOU'RE A FAILURE! I would sabotage things and then try to escape them by lying. Which ultimately made me feel crappy about myself. Now I know. Just own your stuff.

If you're late, don't lie, be honest, and plan better next time. Little lies lead to bigger lies, eating away who you are created to be. If you're telling the truth, you don't have to remember what to say or think so hard to tell your story. Needless to say, I got suspended from school until I could be more responsible, and I just blew off everything I had been striving for in LA.

A big turn-off from that scene was when I went to LA for an "audition with one of my new friends." She said we had to go to the producer's apartment first so they could see if we were the "right look" for a game show host job. The drive was long, and their apartment building looked different from a producer's place. When you haven't had a Father in your life or felt protected by one, you tend to have a blind spot to situations that most people would have red flags.

When we got there, he led my friend into his room, and then I could hear them in there, and she was saying no loud. Boy, did this remind me of being in that car with those boys in Memphis? I stormed into the room, and she was crying as she took off her bra. I knew those two were full of it. I grabbed her, mentioning that these guys were losers and they didn't know anybody there, just trying to get in your pants. That was a big turn-off to the business, for sure. It was time for a new scene and to let go of my acting dreams.

Remember, in chapter three, it was California when I learned about Charlie. I only did three therapy sessions after being curled up in the fetal position when I remembered everything. This all was happening about this time. When we have unresolved stuff, it can manifest in many ways. I became a runner. I would keep myself so busy with stuff I didn't have time to reflect. I would chalk it up to having a good time and living it up. Some girls become slutty to feel loved and worthy. I still had those Christian values I grew up with even though we hadn't attended any church since we left Memphis 2.5 years before. I didn't want to have sex until I got married. I justified a lot of my behavior by holding my V card up as my redeeming factor.

After living in California and starting at the community college, one of my friends from NY moved to California. I was so happy to have a friend that I felt "knew me finally." Close relationships were always important to me because I wasn't raised with siblings, just me and MOM. I missed my family in Arkansas, and Annie was the closest thing to knowing I had come to California. She took me to my first Grateful Dead concert.

I remember wearing a tie-dye and some jean shorts. I couldn't believe it when I got there. The parking lot was full of people with smiling faces. They didn't seem to care about their appearance and were still happy.
See, our identity about how we feel about ourselves mainly comes from our relationship with our Dad. My entire life, I was pretty Polly.

I had been in a few pageants. I never won, but I did a couple. When I came home to England, Arkansas, my Meme would sit me on the pizza freezer in the Dairy Delight. When customers walked in, she would say, "This is my little granddaughter. She's here from Memphis. Isn't she pretty." I held that as my identity. People were free of all that superficial crap in that parking lot, and I loved it. I still wanted to look like I fit in, and I wanted to be the pretty one.

They call the followers Dead Heads. They looked like angels and happy hairy hippie men to me. They were all so loving, and the lot was full of cool vans and fun stuff for sale. The air smelled like patchouli oil and weed and stir fry. There were people blaring music from the dye vans and rainbow colors everywhere. I had a ball. That night after that first show, I was hooked. I said I had to go back. There was a pull I couldn't describe like my tribe was calling me. I felt like they were the new family that loved me exactly where I was, and I didn't need to do anything for them to accept me. Could they like me the way I am?

The next night I had the right look: a long white skirt, a bikini top, and many hippie necklaces. I knew I would be in! I had only smoked pot up to this point and tried cocaine once in New York. This time my friend gave me something called ecstasy.

It was the real deal of MDMA straight from the lab in Texas. The original use was for stage four cancer patients to feel bliss and hopefully release enough serotonin to reverse cancer.

Today they call it Mollie. I am convinced what we had back then was the best, and these pacifier-sucking ravers have no clue. I'm not condoning drug use; I'm just telling you I was part of the original OGs, LOL! I took it and felt a feeling of bliss and freedom I had never felt before. For the first time, I felt free. It was a false sense of freedom, but I didn't care. That was it. I was hooked on that feeling of acceptance and peace. Even if it was partially drug inspired.

My Mom worked so much, and I only had a community college. I would work as a valet parker to earn extra money so I could use it to go on tour. It was super flexible, so I could come and go as I wanted. I used my looks even then to get by with stuff. I always felt somewhat ashamed of being able to get by with more than the other guys could, but I did it anyway.

I remember parking Royal Royce's and getting $100 tips all the time I thought I was rolling. I had two sets of friends: hippie tour friends and skateboarding clubby friends. When I would come home from a tour, I would do both worlds depending on whom I was hanging with.

I still wanted to act when I was home from a tour. I would slip into my club wear and hang out at all the clubs. They had some fantastic clubs in the OC back in the day. I was a good go-go dancer for a few nightclubs when I was home.

I guess I got "discovered in LA." LA was notorious for huge underground warehouse parties, the ORIGINAL raves. Back then, you would get a page on your pager to a pay phone number and a note at the payphone that would lead you to one of these clubs.

One night all the stars from the movie "Breaking" were there. They would have an audience circle them. They would dance in the middle, pump up the crowd, and show all their dance moves.

One night I was pretty fired up, and I knew I was paid by clubs in Newport to dance, so I went for it. I asked my friend, with my newfound cocaine courage, to make a circle around me. The producers from Soul Train were there and asked if I could start dancing on their show. Soul Train was a predominantly black dance show that usually aired on Sunday night for an hour. The dancers were always the coolest, and it would showcase new hip-hop artists. I knew this would be harmless, not like the fake pervert audition I had gone on before. I did it. I filmed on and off for two years.

I had long brown hair to my waist and always wore short jeans, shorts, and usually doc martens. I was one of the only white girls on the show. I never was in the cage on the show. I often wondered why? Then I found out the secret.

The girls with no underwear were featured because the camera crew could get a peep show without anyone knowing, and they could edit that out. I couldn't believe how someone would sell their dignity for fame. Slowly but surely, I realized that not all girls or guys have morals and values. When I was back in Newport after shooting the show, I would mostly hang with my Non-hippie friends. I certainly didn't abide by one of my family's ten commandments.

My Meme would always say it's a lot easier for someone to bring you down than for them to bring you up. If you lie down with dogs, you will get fleas. That just flew right out the window. That's what drugs do: they help you throw caution to the wind and forget the values you know are right.

Cocaine was rampant in SoCal in the late 80s. I had a cocaine dealing boyfriend I would see when I was home. I remember going to his house with cameras all around his house and bodyguards at the door. There were kilos to the ceiling of cocaine. I was still in awe of my drug-dealing Dad, so I would always tell the story of who my Dad worked with. He was Pablo Escobar's pilot in the Iran Contra scandal and was in prison for smuggling 1000 kilos.

I was never raised with my Dad, but I attracted people like him. Trust me, when you don't deal with your Daddy's issues, they will continue to pop up in unhealthy ways. I was never fazed that his house was like this, nor did I feel I was in danger.

Now I know I was constantly testing fate with my no-fear attitude. I had a death wish inside of me from all the pain from the past. That's why I would always push the envelope. God has always protected me.

One night, when I returned from tour, I became the other Polly and went out clubbing all night. When I say tour, I followed the Grateful Dead from town to town with all the other groupie Deadheads.

I was in a destructive downward spiral, and I knew being a hippie on tour was better than this weird feeling of wanting to do cocaine all the time. I like that it kept me from eating, and I could stay skinny. (Such a dumb thing to care about).

When I would go to England growing up, my Grandparents would always say to everyone that came into the Dairy Delight, "Look at my beautiful granddaughter, and she's still a virgin." My outer beauty became a shield to the world where most people couldn't see my inside torment. The external would hide what I felt inside, which became a big motivation always to be obsessed with my looks. This night I was in a house with many spoiled Newport brats.

I locked myself in the bathroom with an eight-ball of blow. I could feel what this stuff was doing to my brain. I felt the feeling of becoming a slave to it. I wrote this poem at nineteen, sitting on the bathroom floor at that party.

THE CUTTING EDGE
written March 11, 1988

I hear the cutting slice as I sit here alone in my corner of the world.

What is it? What is the sound I hear echoing in my mind? The sounds are so loud and in no way to a tunnel of complete darkness!

A ton of light I know is within me of total and complete love.
I know with no altered state of consciousness that I am who I truly am,
But that sounds in the back of my mind begging and pleading why can't I just say no?
Love, what is it? Is it really all within?
Now I'm alone, not lonely, just alone!
I see my Dad in my mind was always searching for light as he did one line after another, constantly searching for himself!
This experience isn't in another white line;
it's inside you; it's in life.
This experience isn't in another white line.
That noise I hear is cutting your life away.
Be a slave to yourself and love and be loved!

I was done with that scene for a while after that night. This was when I moved into full hippie mode. I was doing the two world's shuffle, which was quite familiar to me. After thinking about the love I felt at the few shows I had gone to, I decided to go all in and go on tour full-time. I still had my beautiful gold Jeep and knew a few hippies in town, so I was ready. It was 'No Time to Hate Summer Tour 88.' This was all before the internet.

There was a Grateful Dead phone number we would all call every day to see if days were added for whatever season tour was next. Then in May, they released the summer tour dates and what cities the band would play in. That's when the planning would start. I would ask my little valet spot if I could pick up extra shifts to hit the road with a few hundred dollars. Wow! To travel over 5000 miles and go to over 15 cities and feel secure with only $300 is a miracle.

That summer, I loaded up my Jeep with a cooler in the back and a jam box with a tape deck on the middle counsel, and I was ready to roll. I followed a camper truck with seven people in it, all of whom had been on tour before. I drove alone most of the time, but it was cool. Driving through Nebraska alone is relatively peaceful.

I had my Jeep's top down, my long dreaded hair blowing in the breeze, and my 7-11 big gulp of Dr. Pepper right there. We drove from Newport Beach, Ca. using our atlas to the first show in Alpine Valley, Wisconsin. That was about 1500 miles of mostly freeway. My favorite state was either Wyoming or Nebraska because they were so open and not crowded.

I knew I was home when we pulled into the Alpine Valley recreational center parking lot. The people I came with ditched me, but it didn't matter. I was in my hippie skirt and bikini top, making many friends. The first show was a hot summer night. I brought my half-brother, whom I had never really been around as a kid; he was sixteen with me. We are two and a half years apart in age. His story is that I gave him some party favors, pushed him through the gates, and made him go in. We strolled in and dosed up on whatever we could, and it started raining. I had never felt so free.

I danced naked in the hot rain in the show with all the other naked freaks. It wasn't awkward at all; I was totally free. The heat brought a light summer rain. As the band played, you were the eyes of the world, and people were singing, and everyone was dancing. I felt such joy. When I left the show, I had so much jewelry and items people just gave me throughout the show.

As I walked out, I felt like I was floating. I remember an overwhelming sense of freedom that I had never experienced before. People I didn't even know would approach me and want to sign my skirt. My entire skirt after the tour had so many phone numbers and art on it. I was walking art.

I sold grilled cheese to make money to get to the next show. I could make a whopping $50 on a loaf of bread making those little sandwiches. I drove to six new states and twenty-two more shows. Every state had the same people that were at the show before. It was like miles on the freeways between states with all your new family following you to the next adventure. Every rest stop for 300-500 miles would have hippies playing music and hanging out, traveling in between shows.

The Grateful Dead always played new mixes of their songs at every show. This made every show different. The lead singer Jerry Garcia had a troubled past, and when he would sing, you could feel it in your heart. I felt like I had my Dad. I never had to sing to myself. When he sang Eyes of the World, I saw God looking down on me as a child. I would wake up to find out that you are the eyes of the world! Oh, when I heard that, I felt like I was always cared for by God, even though I had been through a lot as a kid.

After the tour, I drove with a hitchhiker and my little brother down from the east coast to Texas for the rainbow gathering. I met Tom in Wisconsin at a show, and we became bosom buddies. Tom was a rich kid from an elite family in Chicago. He had super fair skin with long brown hair, never wore shoes, and always had his guitar. I always made friends wherever I went.

A rainbow family is a group of like-minded people whose purpose is to create peace wherever they go and educate people about the planet. The big sticker I had on the dashboard of my Jeep was Mother Earth loves you. They have gatherings or do them every July 1-6. They would always pick a national forest somewhere in the country, deep in the woods.

No money was exchanged; they entirely depended on the barter system. People would create kitchens, and food was free; you bring your own bowl and utensils. It was amazing to be in the middle of a forest and even have pizza sometimes. On July 4, everyone would gather around the fire and drum circle. They would hold hands and meditate on world peace for 30 minutes. Imagine every type of person and culture gathered over 3-4,000 people holding hands and meditating on peace.

As we pulled up, my hair from riding over 4000 miles with my Jeep's top off was almost blonde. My skin was brown like a cocoa bean, and my hair was almost dreads. I lost 20 lbs. on tour and now weigh about 108 lbs. At 5'7", that's small. Everyone, there was saying I look over your family. This was the first time I had seen something like this. I missed my family in Arkansas and had a longing inside to be connected to people.

After three nights of being there and sleeping in whoever's tent, I knew I was sick. I had slept on the ground, in my car, at random hotels for over a month, and I was spun out. I made it to town, an hour's hike out of the woods and another hour's drive to civilization.

I found a pay phone and called my Mom collect. I said, "Momma come get me; everybody left me that would have driven back to Cali with me." Of course, Esther Jean flew on the next plane there! I saw my Mom and just collapsed in her arms. I was so exhausted and had the beginning of malaria.

We checked into a hotel, and I soaked in the tub for 2 hours. The water was black and smelled like feet. My Mom disinfected my car and ensured she wouldn't get scabies by riding in it. We left like Thelma and Louis and drove through the hottest part of the country in that Jeep home. My Mom always has been my Rock. She was Mom and Dad.

When we returned to Newport, I rested and went back to school, still hippie out and barefoot. By September, it was time for the fall tour. I rested my bones, and it was time to return to Trucking on (yes, that's another Dead song called Trucking). The guy we moved to Cali for had disappeared, and Mom was working for a new company and thinking of starting her own business. We were both growing and experiencing new things. I felt safest when I was running, that's for sure.

Fall tour came, I loaded my little Jeep up and went off. The drive from Newport to Northern California was only seven hours, so it was the perfect distance. Santa Cruz was the hippie meet-up spot on the west coast, and that's where I first met Ryan (now my hubby). I had never told anyone about my Dad until I told him. I just trusted him from the be- ginning and felt a deep connection that I knew I was safe with him.

We would run into each other at shows and dance together but never kissed. These shows were in

September, and after they were over, I went back to Newport and waited for the winter tour in December. Winter tour was here, and that's where I met the guy to whom I would give my precious V card to.

It was the Long Beach Show in 1988, only an hour from my house. We were dancing inside the shows on massive amounts of ecstasy, and I heard a flute. This magical creature was playing flute wearing all white, playing to all the spinning deadheads. He had long wavy brown hair, piercing blue eyes, and a scraggly beard. Of course, I immediately connected with him. That night I went home and told my Mom I met someone, and he was staying in the desert, and he was **the one**.

I was so lost, and my head spun from doing drugs. Charles Manson could have come along; I might have thought the same thing. Three days later, I got in my little gold Jeep and drove to the high desert. I drove for 30 minutes on a dirt road after I got off the freeway past giant boulders, broken down clunky cars, and old metal homes that looked like a third-world country. At nineteen, I was still innocent, naive, and trusting of everyone.

I pulled up to Indri's place (that was my newfound hippie love name). It was his friend's hideout; this was his convicted felon fugitive pad. Hmmm, sound familiar? I picked a familiar situation, like my Dad.

When I pulled up to the lean he was staying in, they attached a broken-down school bus to the house to make extra rooms. This is where we were going to sleep. That was the night I gave my virginity away. I had saved it all these years and wanted to save it for marriage. I gave it up to a druggy, Charles Manson-looking homeless hippie in a rusted broken-down school bus attached to a lean shack in the desert. WOW! To a man who was thirteen years older than me and homeless, and somehow I thought was enlightened and a high spiritual guru.

Wow, please take my older self-advice to save yourself. Your virginity is your prized possession; you can't get it back once it's gone. I woke up and felt dirty and ashamed, even in my spaced-out brain. I knew that was a gross way to give up something so special.

I drove back home about three hours away to So Cal and told my Mom I would go to college in Santa Cruz. She was sad, but I was finished at community college. In the middle of drugs, hippies, cocaine, and tour, God gave me the grace to get my AA degree. No, there were no online classes. I physically had to be there.

When you have an unsettling in your spirit, man, you always have this push inside of you. I knew I was messing up in some areas, but to prove I was still ok, I would accomplish things so I could not feel like a total loser. I still do that to this day.

As I wrote this book sitting in quarantine for the past seven weeks, I knew it was time for it. I can see that little girl always trying to prove she wasn't a loser, still pushing through. I have tools known to help, but it's always there.

It was Christmas time. I left right after Christmas with all my beautiful clothes in the Jeep. I started staying in my new boyfriend's van with all his friends outside Berkeley, waiting to go to Santa Cruz for school in January. We pulled into Oakland to the new year's show, and I heard a bang on the van asking for Polly Angel. That was my hippie name. It was Ryan. He hadn't seen me since all this had transpired. He said you have to come with me.

We walked through the parking lot, and he gave me a card and told me to wait to read it until he left. He told me I was ruining my life hanging with these losers. I just thought he was pushy, and I ignored him. I went back to the van and read the card. It said he had never felt our connection, which was real. He signed it. I love Ryan. Not I love you. So I said well, he loves himself. I didn't see him anymore until twenty-five years later. That is part of my beautiful next book.

Part of not having a Dad or experiencing the love of a Father is that you sometimes need better judgment or discernment in situations. That's what Dads do; they help you feel secure and teach you about the world from a man's perspective so you can have discernment and make wise choices to help you get out of harm's way. I wish I would have known then what I know now. Of course, if I did, I wouldn't have gone through all the trials I put myself through, and I wouldn't be writing this book. Maybe I would, but it would be a lot more boring. Remembering all this craziness could have been a life filled with joy, not just wild adventures where I could have gotten harmed or even died. It's all good life's a journey, not a destination.

Indre and I parked in San Francisco that night, and I, with my naivety and probably drug-induced stupidity, left all my stuff from Christmas in the car. I never thought about the thieves. I was still on a high from the shows we just left. Most people were good. The following day, I got up, and all my clothes were gone. My Mom bought me stuff from Niemen Marcus for Christmas, and my beautiful clothes were all gone.

She wanted me to remember the nice things in life to reel me back out of that hippie phase. I remember getting up the following day, and everything was gone. I saw bums on the street wearing $1000 jackets. I got a few things back, but most of it was gone. My Mom had lost her contract with the company she was working for right before Christmas that year. I didn't know how broke we were. Despite everything, she spent the last bit of money she had to ensure I had a great Christmas that year. That one was a hard pill to swallow. She didn't tell me that till years later.

That was it. I left the bay area to return to Newport to tell my Mom goodbye one more time before I took off to school in Santa Cruz. At this point, Indre was my boyfriend. My Mom had no idea I already gave up my V card in a dilapidated school bus to him. I had to go pick him up in the desert where it, the fabulous first time, had all happened because that was where he was staying while he waited for me. I wanted to take him to Santa Cruz with me, so my Mom came with me to get him. Her real reason for riding up to BFE was to protect me from Charles Manson (that's what she called him). OMG, the things I've put my Mom through.

My Mom jumped in the Jeep, and we drove to the high desert on a beautiful sunny, cold California day. We drove past all those dilapidated jalopies and hillbilly deliverance lean-to-shacks on that dirt road until we finally got to a ranch in the middle of the high desert. It looked like the Beverly hillbillies before they got rich; let's say that. We got there at nightfall, and she was a sport. The only place to sleep was a pool table, so we did. My sweet Mom sleeping in the middle of what they called the den, which was really the only room in the shack, was a trip. The only source of warmth was the wood-burning stove in the corner. It wasn't the Ritz, that's for sure.

The next morning, she went hiking with us to the naked hot springs in the valley. She was bound and determined not to let me be alone with this guy. She knew she was in for a hike to the hot springs. This gorgeous place in the high desert is called Deep Creek Hot Springs. They are naturally occurring hot springs. They sit perched on the side of a mountain and look like little pools next to a raging river. They're warm because of the hot lava that's underneath the ground. You have to hike about a mile and a half down a cliff and cross over an icy river to get there. In the winter, it's still cold in the high desert in California, and the river has ice on it usually. Here's the kicker, you have to go naked across the river so you don't get your clothes wet to get in the hot springs.

Esther would ensure I didn't go across that river with that boy alone. So she hiked all the way, took her clothes off, left them on the beach, got naked, and went across that icy river with a Charles Manson look-alike. She got in the hot spring and made sure she sat in between both of us and finished off a bottle of champagne with him and me.

She said when she looked at him naked, standing over the river with something sticking out, she was running across that river to make sure he didn't get near me with that thing. I was nineteen, and my Mom was about forty-five. That was the fastest I ever saw my Mom do anything. She beat both of us up the cliff, put her clothes on, and just dashed out of there. She never lets me forget that she remembers how great she felt after the Hot Spring experience.

That was it. I took my Mom home, said my goodbyes, and was off again. Indre and I dropped mushrooms on our trip up Highway Five, about an eight-hour drive to Santa Cruz. Some of the hippie crap he wrote was so beautiful he inspired me to start writing more creatively. I even have a copy of a poem that I wrote on the magical ride to Santa Cruz.

It's called:

Turn your frown upside down

Rain is pouring down on me
I guess I'm right where I'm supposed to be.
It looks like I'm doing all right
My home is right here in my heart
Could this be the place where I should start?
I'm Flapping my wings for the first time.
How am I doing?
Am I soaring like an eagle,
or am I falling like a newfound dove?
What are these feelings?
Could this be love?
I feel it all around it.
It's turned my life upside down.
It looks like I'm doing all right
So take the seeds of fear and doubt and yes,
throw them right out into eternity and
let yourself just be eternally free!!

Is that some Hippie crap, or what? I wish I could find him, but I've heard he passed away. He wrote the most beautiful book called "The Adventures of Tickle Bug Love in Giggly." If anyone knows him and they read this, his name was Ronald Humberg. He always would carry his art pouch and all of his writings, and he wrote the most beautiful story I've ever heard. I cried for three hours on the drive to Northern California, just thinking about what a beautiful story it was.

It was a story about love and inclusion, which we could all use in our life right now. Even if the messenger is wrong, you can always find a message that you can use for good. When we first got to Santa Cruz, Indre and I slept in the Jeep many nights and in hotel rooms on the floor at people's places. I acted like I was a homeless person looking back. That was so weird. I was supposed to start college but was too hippy out and having too much fun, like sitting on the Santa Cruz mall panhandling for money and then going dumpster diving to get leftover organic fruits and vegetables, or standing by the mall pay phone, waiting to see when the Grateful Dead would release their following tour dates.

I was crazy trying to convince myself even to attempt to go to school up there. My total obsession was just to run away. With all the drugs and all the fun I was having, I could physically escape everything that was happening inside of me. It was easier back then, but boy, does all your baggage raise its nasty head later in life if you don't handle it when you're younger.

I saw Ryan a few times in Santa Cruz, but we didn't hang out much because now I had this guy in my life, and he called him the wrecking crew. I knew I couldn't go to school in the winter. I was too spun out. So we all hippies bought one-way flights to Hawaii, the Big Island. I had not even a dollar in my pocket and only a backpack, and I was determined to go live off the land with all the other Hippies.

I was searching for what my father was telling me about in the letters he would write from prison. See, while my Dad was a fugitive, and when he was on the run, he lived in Hawaii part-time. He lived there, bought a property, and grew weed under another alias, Lucas Harmony. He took my little brother, my little sister, and my stepmom. She's the one that helped him fake his suicide and led the feds down a different path for years so that my Dad could escape and go set up a spot for them.

When my Dad came back to life, that put another nail in the coffin for my self-esteem, that's for sure. Like why did he take my half-brother and sister and not me? What was wrong with me? I even held a grudge against my Mom for years. I thought because she left him, I didn't have a relationship.

Now I know that was total crap. My Mom never really told me at this point all the horrific things he had done to her before and during their marriage. That's what we sometimes do to protect that child inside of us that feels abandoned. We blame the parent that sticks it out because we know they won't leave. Rejection has nothing to do with you when you're a child of not being good enough. It has everything to do with the other person's inability to keep their word and selfishness.

I knew that my father had a property in Hawaii, and I was desperate to find out any pieces of who this man was. My Mom had never really told me all the horrific things he had done; she just let me find out my things on my own. She waited until I was older and needed to tell me the truth. I began to idolize my Dad. I thought he was some real hero, a gangster that flew drugs for the cartel and Pablo Escobar.

I remember once being at the Warfield in San Francisco, it was a Jerry Garcia band show, and I had my little Jeep that didn't lock. I was high as a kite in the parking lot and missed the show and put myself in the car and put the covers over my head. Everybody knew my Dad had people after him, and the best place I could hide was with the Grateful Dead Hippies.

While lying in the back of my Jeep, I heard two men saying this is the Betzner car. We need to find her. I curled up tighter in a ball and slowed my breath so they wouldn't know I was there. Finally, after I knew they were gone, I asked everyone if they saw any strange characters in the lot. They said there were two dudes in long trench coats that looked Colombian.

Come to find out, they were two guys from Columbia that the cartel sent to kidnap me and hold me for ransom so that my Dad would not rat them out in prison. God has always protected and watched over me, even in my craziness, because that's what kind of Father He is.

Back to my story Indre and I got on the plane with twenty other Hippies and took our one-way flight to Hawaii. We landed in Hawaii, and one of my Dad's friends picked us up. He was a groovy granola-type guy who was all about natural health and took us to a park. We pulled up, and beautiful people danced, glowing, natural, earthy people everywhere, waving flags, holding sarongs, and eating coconuts. That park and a tent became my home for the next few months. I would get up in the morning with all the hippies and go foraging in the woods for our food. We would collect pineapples, avocados, and mangoes and eat like gluttons all day.

One day we went to a friend's place nearby, where they had a hidden cave on their property. As we hiked through the woods back to this cave, I remember looking at the ground and thinking nothing couldn't be in there. As the guy slowly pushed back a piece of plywood, I looked inside. A ladder and steam were coming out of the hole. I said let's go for it. I hiked down into the hole, and there was a beautiful cavern filled with candles and Hot Springs as far as you could see. It was glorious. We soaked for the day. I had never seen anything so beautiful and mysterious.

The longer I was there in Hawaii, the more Indris alcoholism took over, and the more I knew I was just doing a babysitting job that would end eventually. Hawaii was one of the significant places to grow marijuana globally, but it was not legal yet. When Harvest would come in for the light Depp's in April, all the farmers would throw all of the trim and leaves into giant garbage bags and throw them in the trash. Like good hippies, we would collect all the trash bags, about twenty 55-gallon bags full of weed.

I had no idea what we would do with all that, but Indre sure did. We drove back in the middle of the woods to this communal intentional living farm.

I remember distinctly how everyone there talked about how we would make hash oil. I had never seen Hash oil to me. They said this would be a 24-hour process and that we'd all need to stay awake the entire time. In my little head, I thought I was off cocaine, and I had no idea how I could stay awake for hours and work to make this hash oil.

Suddenly this throwback from Woodstock days, a guy from the 60s opened his freezer. We all looked on with amazement as he had saved a hit of acid since 1971 called yellow sunshine. It had 5000 microdots in one hit. One hit of acid today is about 100 micrograms, which is the usual dose people take to partake in that kind of drug. Do the math on that one?

So he split it five ways, meaning I did 1000 mcg, which would be 100 hits of acid today. I had no idea what I was in for; let's just say I stayed awake for a very long time. When I started tripping all the Woodstock throwbacks, I loaded up into a Tacoma truck and drove to Millionaire's Pond.

This was this acre-wide hundred-degree pond right next to the ocean. When you pulled up, you could hear frogs because, remember, it's a freshwater pond in the middle of nowhere right next to the ocean in the middle of nowhere. You could hear waves crashing over the cliffs coming down the side into the water. The sound was glorious, especially with my heightened sense of awareness. The next thing I knew, I was a frog. I thought I was a frog, jumping into the water and croaking just like a frog for hours. We stayed there for hours and hours and played. I was a mermaid. I was a frog. I was an aquatic animal.

I am confident I morphed into every single character you can imagine. It took me a few days to get my words back to where I could speak English again. I can't believe God fixed my brain, and that didn't fry me forever, but it was an experience I would never forget.

We had hitchhiked around the island because we didn't have a car and ended up staying with one of his friends on the other side. I had severe mosquito bites as they had eaten my legs and arms, and my boyfriend was too drunk to help me. We stayed at this thrift store in the back room, and I remember his friend putting something all over my body and a lot of aloes and helping me to put my brain back together and heal my bites. I knew I needed to return to the island's other side.

My only contact with my Mom was I could call her from a pay phone once a week, but she had no way to contact me. I had no phone, no address, and I knew she must've been worried sick. I had been there for about 3 to 4 months, and one night, we went to another commune on the ocean. I saw a friend of mine I had not seen in years. Her name was Heart Weaver, and she was about the same age as me. I was not walking with the Lord, but He was always walking with me.

This young lady had no idea about my situation, nor did she know my Mom was the only birth parent involved in my life. She had no idea I had such a close relationship with her. I only knew her from dancing in the hallways on tours back in the States.

She walked me through the forest, sat me on the side of the cliff, and she said, "I have a message. I had no idea who it was for, but now I know it's for you." She said, "As I was sitting here facing California's coast, I can see a woman sitting in California on the coast screaming her daughter's name. Polly, come home; call me!" She said, "Are you from California?" I said yes. She said, "Does your mother have red hair?" I said yes. She said, "You have to go home. She is calling you crying on the beach."

The following day, I called my Mom from a payphone at the only store on that side of town. She was crying when she answered the phone because I had not called her in weeks. I could hear her crying, which I didn't hear often; She said, "Polly, you got to come home."

I got on a plane that day and flew home. The experience of seeing my Mom was like when I landed in her arms when she came to get me after I had been at the rainbow gathering and had malaria. My little face was fat like a chipmunk from all of the fruits and vegetables I had been eating off the land, and I was brown as a cocoa bean.

She had started her Association and was becoming more successful. She knew California would never be good for me, and I would continue on this path. The man that she had come there for dis- appeared, and she had no way to find him, and she was devastated. We both missed our family in the South. So my Mom and I sat down one night and talked. We opened up an atlas map, and she said close your eyes and pick. I closed my eyes and picked and pointed to Atlanta, Georgia. Neither of us had ever lived there, but our family was still in Arkansas and Memphis, so we knew that that was it.

Atlanta was only a seven-hour drive, and that was way closer than a two-day drive, that's for sure. Within two weeks, we packed up all our belongings and were off. Polly and Esther drive across the country to move back to the South. My wild little stent in California was over, and we were back in the South.

Chapter 7

ATLANTA SOUTHERN FRIED FUN MISSIONARY DATING PART 2

I get it. We all need the freedom to temporarily escape this misery that we call Earth until we finally get our real freedom in heaven. The book of Romans says, 'We have all fallen short of the glory of God.' I often meditated on that verse when I was little. I didn't know what it meant. Now I know it means there is such freedom you can experience when you know how much God, your Heavenly Father loves you. You get that running anyway, except you learn that trying to stand against Him is like trying to spit in the wind. It's unfulfilling and usually ends up causing a lot more grief than joy which was never God's plan for your life.

Any good father only wants happiness and joy for His kids. That's why the realization that I always had a Heavenly Father that had always been looking out for me gave me the peace inside myself that I am enough the way I am and the way I'm not. I'm OK! Even though I finally uprooted the deep seeded pain inside myself during my hippie California days, I still had not been restored to my original settings, let's say that. In Atlanta, I just reset to my default settings: to put on a happy face, go on an adventure, and don't think about why I get into some really hairy situations. My default settings also show why I choose things that could hurt me and lead me down a dark path. My default was to sabotage the good in my life so that I could fulfill that little girl's thoughts that she wasn't good enough! That's what we do when we are in pain. We challenge life and situations and push the envelope.

Atlanta was a new freedom. All my Cali and New York experience gave me a leg up over most Southern people. I knew I could open up to people in the South to see things more like I did, which was way more relaxed and fun! Now looking back, I am arrogant and immature.
Esther and I got to Atlanta in the summertime.

We moved into this fantastic hotel with an indoor pool. I remember we would go to this cute little restaurant, and I must've had two chocolate milkshakes a day. I gained 15 pounds the first month we were there. I quickly lost that. Let me tell you. We moved into this darling little house, and I had the whole upstairs. It was brick and had two stories. We had a beautiful yard with many dogwoods. It was on a cul-de-sac with other lovely traditional homes. The home was in a typical suburban neighborhood in the South.

I felt lonely but was so happy to return to the South because I knew my grandparents, aunts, uncles, and cousins were only seven hours away.

I wanted a dog, so we went to the Humane Society, and I saw the most precious half Labrador, half chow little solid black fur ball puppy. Of course, I named him Cassidy after my third favorite grateful dead song. My Mom was becoming more successful, and I knew I had to get it together.

One of the weekends, she went out of town. I went to a Hippie concert downtown, and a nice older man there asked if he could stay at my home because it was going to be raining, and he needed a place to stay. And my dumb self said, of course, you could come to stay at my house. I did not know this guy was homeless, so my little puppy and I were hanging out in the house, and the next thing I knew, his giant dog attacked my puppy and bit his eyeball out. I was horrified. I couldn't believe something so wrong happened, but I forgave the man and asked him to please leave. At that point, I was horrified

Sweet Cassidy!

I took Cassidy in my lap alone to the vet to see if they could save his little eye. They couldn't save it. I felt terrible, like, why did my compassion have to cause my innocent dog pain?

My Mom came home the next day, and we both decided that being home wasn't a great plan. So we ran an ad in the local paper for a roommate for the college in Athens where UGA is. I knew I was going to go to the University of Georgia, which is only an hour away from Atlanta which after my Mom and I being so codependent, moving all the way back together wasn't too far.

An awesome lady answered the ad, and I got to go meet her daughter. She was cool and pretty and fun. Her mom just did not want her to have roommates from her high school when she went to growing up she wanted someone new. So off we went. Our rent was $500 for a two-bedroom, two-bath townhouse on the outskirts of town. It was perfect. I was still in my hippie phase and wasn't missionary dating yet. I had only met a few people.

The best friend I made, I sat on her when I was getting on the bus to go to class, and we are still best friends to this day. God always gives us little blessings in ways that sometimes we don't even ask, but we do need. That's what Dads do: they know what you need before you need it and then make sure they try their best to give it to you. Me and Alison, our second night hanging out. She was always the cool one!

Oh my goodness, the adventures with Allison were hilarious. She was a punk rocker, and I was a hippie. We were bound for great things. Not even five months after we met, I talked her into going to a rainbow gathering in deep Florida. Right when we got there, she connected with these dudes named Snot and Trash.

They were the only punk rockers there. She was so shocked about the naked hairy hippies that she had to find something in common with somebody there. We got super close during that little adventure, so we decided to return home, load up, and return for another adventure. I wanted to go down to Tampa to see my sister for spring break just a month after our last adventure, but I didn't know her that well, and she's my half-sister. I call her one of the OGs (original Gary's).

Allison and I always had so much fun, and she also liked to push the boundaries. On our way to Tampa from Atlanta was about a nine-hour drive, so we decided it would be a good idea to drink a whole bottle of Robitussin. If you've ever done such a crazy thing, it makes you wholly lucid and almost like an LSD trip.

I do not suggest you do this or condone it. I didn't care about the outcome. I was just in the moment and certainly didn't think about how things could go south. God (my real Dad) always protected me from my insanity! While high as a kite on our trip, we had a brilliant idea to go to a bar we didn't know that it was a gay alternative bar. I just wanted to show off the dance moves I learned in Cali on Soul Train.

When we pulled up in front of the club, I said, "Alison, do soul-train dancers wear leather?" I thought I saw a man with a giant afro peeping through the sunroof when we pulled up. Come to find out, I was staring at Alison's leather jacket, and her arm morphed into a soul-train dancer. Let's just say I had no idea what I was talking about because I was hallucinating that there were dancers from soul train in front, but they were actually new waivers white gay men. We left because we were laughing so hard that we couldn't even distinguish genres of music or what people actually looked like. If we stayed, we probably would have gotten beat up, gone to jail, or gone to the loony bin.

Young and dumb, we didn't think too far in advance, so we didn't have a place to sleep that night. As any intelligent young person does, we headed to the local park. I looked in the park, and just as seriously as all get out, I said, "Allison, oh my gosh, look. This giant field has tons of trash bags, so we can just sleep here."

She thought it was a great idea too. As we got closer, they started moving for a minute. We both thought we were hallucinating hard again. Then we realized it was bodies sleeping everywhere. It was a park full of homeless people; how perfect. We found a blowup bed in our car, blew it up in the park, and slept with all the homeless people. How nothing happened that night is a miracle. That's what I mean your heavenly Father always protects you even when you don't protect yourself.

The following day, we continued driving and went down to see my sister. I was quite a daredevil most of the time and loved pushing the envelope. We walked into a tattoo parlor because Alison and I both wanted to get tattoos, and so did my sister. We felt it was something perfect as a memory of our crazy adventure. I was lying on the table with my butt in the air, ready for my first tattoo. Allison elbowed me, and she said, "Polly, look at his T-shirt." The man about to mark me for life had "at least one dream came true" on the front of his T-shirt with a picture of Martin Luther King dead and blood everywhere. I'm not a racist, so I wanted to freak these rednecks out. It's a brilliant thing to think of doing when someone is about to give you art that you will have for life on your body. I told him, ", Wow, this place is really cool," to open up the dialogue with him.

He asked me if I was single, so I, with my smart mouth, said no, I'm not single. I have a really amazing boyfriend named Tyrone. I felt him choke in his throat, and he said, "Tyrone, what kind of name is that?" I said that's my African-American boyfriend, a defensive lineman for the Tampa Bay Buccaneers. He just about threw up in his mouth and said, "We don't really like your kind of people around here. I'm one racist FR." these were his exact words. I said, "Well, that's just fine, just give me my tattoo."

Well, I still have that tattoo, and I guess the joke on me because after years and years of wondering why sometimes I had bad luck, now I know. The moon and star on my booty were supposed to be cute, but it looks just like Isis's symbol. Oh my gosh, did we laugh about that one for days? I look at that, and I just think I was so lucky it didn't come out even worse. Allison chose not to get her tattoo there because she was smart, and we headed back to Atlanta.

After six months of hardly attending class, I got all F's that entire semester. I found a few friends that could go on the Grateful Dead tour with me. I knew to go to my game plan, which was to keep on Trucking. I knew that feeling I had on tour and in Hawaii of being free from any pain and memories of my past, and if I could go to that place inside, I could keep pushing all my issues down. Trust me; they rear their ugly head eventually. You can run, but you can't hide.

I packed up my little Jetta because I left the Jeep in Cali, and there we went. The guy I had a crush on and three other people in my little car, and we were hitting the shows.

After the first night, the guy I had a crush on, let's just call him R, and I finally got together. I was so happy I had a long-haired hippie boyfriend, but of course, he sold weed on the side and was just a repeat of what I had always picked. He was probably something like what I thought my Dad must be like.

We were all running out of money, so we decided to drive back down to Georgia and go mushroom picking in the middle of the night. Like that's a good idea, I go pushing that envelope again. We must've picked five pounds of mushrooms, dried them out, and drove back up to Chicago for a thirteen-hour drive. We had three pounds of mushrooms, all broken up into quarter bags of 180 quarters. Just do the math. We sold every quarter at 40 bucks a pop. I made $ 8000 in one day.

The show was terrific at Soldier Field, and was the most gorgeous stadium. When we came out of the show, we had tons of people sitting on the roof of our car. My first thought was that they wanted more. Here's the kicker: we didn't try the mushrooms before we sold them, and half of them were no good.

We did plenty of refunds that night, trust me. We all walked away with about $5000, which ended the summer tour. We didn't want anyone else to see our faces, so we returned to Athens. God always protected me, even when I was an idiot. We could have really gotten a beating!

I was hoping R would become my knight in shining armor. We had a little apartment in downtown Athens. It was above a bar, and we lived with my best friend, Alison. The living situation could have been more conducive to studying. After a year, we moved to Atlanta. We got a little apartment, and I talked him into cutting his hair off and getting a job at a "normal place." People only change when they want to. If you try to get someone to conform before they are ready, you become a classic missionary dater. So if you are reading this, do you do this? Like in your relationships, do you say, "Well, I know he or she can change because I love them so much?"

Only one thing can change a person, and that's a real Savior, and we aren't that. We are humans. Yes, we need to see people at their potential and guide them in the right direction. This doesn't mean we date them to get them there! He was miserable trying to be something that he wasn't. I wanted so badly for my love to be enough to change him. He had his own issues to work through, and I was trying to force him. I worked as a cocktail waitress at different bars with my best friend, Allison. She was back home trying to make money too. We did some pretty hilarious pictures, one of which sold for $10,000 to an Aids project and is currently still hanging on a lesbian bar in Atlanta, No, we were not lesbians, but we posed as if we were for charity.

My life was just full of craziness. I didn't know my boyfriend's addiction had hit an all-time high. Yep, repeat number two; this time, it was drugs. I thought that with enough love and enough loyalty behind him, I could change him to make him who I wanted him to be. I did a course called Lifespring, and when they asked what drugs I'd done in the past three months, I raised my hand for pretty much everything. I was just casually doing stuff here and there. I didn't think it was a problem. So she asked me if I had a death wish. I never even thought of that. I just thought I was having a good time, but maybe deep down, I didn't really care if I lived or died. The leader from that course was another angel sent to make me take a step back. Start looking at your life and remember those people put in your path to help you; they are angels sent from heaven to guide you and get you back on your real path.

My Mom was living about 2 miles away from R and me. I just wasn't really telling her everything. I was always searching for what was making me tick inside because I knew something was holding me back and making me fail. She knew the only way to get me out of this toxic relationship was to put a carrot in front of me. She wanted to try to help me remember where I came from. She thought that if I moved home, I should be in the Miss Georgia pageant. We would call all the people I grew up with at Federal Express and at different businesses she knew, and they could be sponsors. So now I have moved home, and my boyfriend is living by himself, and we were trying to figure it out. The Miss Georgia Pageant came, and I felt beautiful. I just needed to be more politically correct to win. By this time, my Hippie self-had morphed into my club self, and slowly but surely, my boyfriend and I we're breaking up. Since I moved back to my Moms, my ex had a close friend die in our apartment just three months after I moved out. R went right back to the long hair bar guy. That was where he was on his journey.

We are still friends, and if I haven't apologized to you, R here, it is. I'm so sorry I tried to change you and didn't accept you right where you were. I wanted the fairy tale to be enough to make you change into my prince charming to mend those Daddy scars I had inside of, not feeling like I was enough. You were such a sweet man to me, and I'll never forget that summer together. You are a precious person who always had such ingenious ideas and compassion. I hope you'll forgive me if I hurt you in any way. God bless you.

Summer 1991 Tour

Chapter 8

MEETING HUBBY #1

That Christmas R and I ended things. It wasn't pretty, he was so sad about his friend dying, and I left too, but I knew it was the right time. I had started on a new path. I started to model again. I got a job with Miller, and I was a Miller Cold Patrol Girl and many other liquor companies. I would go to bars and see if guys wanted to buy beer or whatever alcohol I was representing that day, and I would have to be sexy enough to make them want it. I didn't have any control over the storm inside of me, but I could control my exterior, so I focused on that.

My hair was super long and full again, and I was tan and skinny I felt great (sort of). Looks aren't everything, but I thought that would make me happy at that point in my life. Remember, as a kid, I was Pretty Polly. If you look good on the outside, then you must be fine on the inside. Looks were always my go-to. Thank God I was cute again!

I started dating a few people, one of which was the manager for Boyz II Men, the band, and he was about 15 years older than me and had a few Ferraris. He was loaded and way different than any guy I had ever dated. He was just a little too normal for me (and old). I needed something wild again. In other words, he was healthy and wanted to care for and cherish me. I wasn't healed of my wounds yet and couldn't accept someone like that.

I was now working for Jim Beam, and they hired me to go in a limo and ride from Atlanta to Athens to do a Jim Beam promotion. They would have me sign autographs and Jim Beam bottles for all the football players and everyone who came to the event after a Georgia game. Kim, one of my good friends, and I, who I'm still friends with today, said she wanted me to meet someone again. I had already met him before, but I needed to remember. I met him lying on her floor looking at lasers on the ceiling, but it was more in my hippy days the first time I lived in Athens. This guy was all about the superficial TNA. That's what he wanted, and back then, I was not that.

Now I was TNA, and it was time to re-meet my first husband. Now this story is pretty hilarious. I was doing a Jim Beam promotion, and there were 100 guys in line paying to do shots off my stomach. Theodore cut in line and said, "You don't need to do this anymore, and you need to come sit in my lap." So I did, and the rest was history. We spent that whole night together, and we partied like rock stars. We danced to the NY NY song, and I told him I would marry him that night.

Pretty gutsy on a first date, but somehow I knew! I knew I would never be back with R again, and somehow I thought this one would work out. I remember trying to be practical in my mind in my early 20s. I thought his parents were still married after 40 years, he was in college, and I felt like he was somewhat normal.

Remember, I still hadn't really done any therapy since I was in California. I was just going through life on autopilot. I was still living at home in Atlanta, and he was in Athens. I was modeling for different companies and one of the companies decided that if I was going to make plenty of money doing NASCAR, I needed to get my boobs done, so they paid for it. Theodore and I weren't totally exclusive yet, and I was still seeing a Ferrari guy.

When I was healing at my house, he brought Boys II Men to sing in my living room to make me feel better. My Mom was shocked she couldn't even believe it. This colossal band was serenading me in my Mom's living room like a 20 by 20 space.

The next day Theodore came, and I said goodbye to Mr. Ferrari guy. I went for partying with a college guy over a stable, than a rich guy who adored me. I often wonder what my life would've been like if I had just accepted someone who was somewhat normal and treated me with honor and respect. Life's a journey, not a destination.

When you grow up knowing your Dad loves you and he protects you, you tend to have a much better discernment and a better selector, that's for sure. When you still need to work out your Daddy Issues, you pick someone to help you facilitate the process. Little did I know he was more like my Dad than I thought, very manipulative like my father. He knew how to turn things and twist things to make me feel like everything was always my fault and I was crazy.

I would drive back and forth from Athens to Atlanta to see him every weekend and work in between. I am going to college in Atlanta now. After doing Lifespring, I knew I wanted to pursue a degree in art. When I was at UGA, I was going into psychology, which was a path that worked for me. I wanted to do fashion merchandising and marketing now.

After only dating for two weeks, I entered the Miss Howard Stern contest. He is a radio personality that, let's just say, he pushes the envelope. I entered the contest in Georgia and won for the whole state. There we were, a new couple flying to NYC for the contest. I guess there was no accident on our first date we danced to the song NY. When we landed and got to the hotel, I was shocked. The guy who got his penis cut off by his wife was a judge. They had sado-masochists that were their talent, naked lesbian Congo players. The list went on and on.

Theodore was in heaven; this was pure craziness at another level. The producers wanted me to do some nasty act as my talent, and I wasn't down for that. I pretended to be sick, and we explored the city and fell in love. I knew I was going to marry him. OK, if you're with a guy who flies to a circus act freak show after only dating for two weeks and thinks it's kinky and cool, RUNNNNNN!

One weekend after a few days of wild parties and late nights, I felt sick and couldn't sleep. We had been dating for five weeks, and one morning I woke up, and I was bleeding profusely. I had no idea what was happening. I had not had a period in about six weeks. I told him I thought I needed to go to the hospital. He rushed me to the hospital, and I was hemorrhaging. I was six weeks pregnant, so it could not have been his baby. I was pregnant with twins, and I was having a miscarriage.

Holy crap, I'm with the guy I think is the ONE, and now I'm pregnant with another man's baby!! I was horrified and expected him to bounce. What sealed the deal was that he stuck with me during the process.

He said, "I don't want you to tell your ex anything. I'll go through this with you, and we'll be fine." I've never felt comfort from a man like that, so I felt like he must be the ONE!!

Experiences like that bond you with people, but you need to know exactly what is bonding you with someone. If I look at the whole situation from my perspective, I was whacked. I was bonding with a man because he cared about me and didn't want to lose me even though I was pregnant with somebody else's baby that wasn't his, and I was having a miscarriage. Pretty messed up reason to bond with anyone.

A healthy relationship isn't riddled with such drama too often from the beginning. How a relationship starts is usually a good indication of how it will keep going. I wasn't used to peace, and drama seemed normal to me. I just kept believing if God brought me to it, He would bring me through it. Even though my life was a Godless mess, I always knew I could ask God to guide me.

The moment you step out into it, "It seems right." The territory is when you walk away from the truth, and life goes sideways. It seems the right philosophy usually is a path to death (not necessarily actual death but your real path, death, the one God intended for you). Truth is the opposite of that. The devil comes and gets you off the path in three ways:

1. Deception
2. Accusation
3. Persecution

I'm pretty sure this whole situation was deception, but God always works what was meant for evil for good. I had a miscarriage, and we stayed together, and our life was crazy and totally Godless, not going to church or any part of God in our life except maybe an occasional prayer when we were fighting.

At that time, I lived in Atlanta and would drive back and forth to see him on the weekends. I was in school in Atlanta and finally graduated and got my degree. He graduated about six months into our relationship, and he moved to Atlanta, and we got a small apartment. Life was crazy. He was doing things that won't be mentioned in the book because I don't have his permission to, but let's say some things weren't part of his job description when he graduated from college.

After my boob job, NASCAR hired me to do all kinds of gigs where I would sign autographs at different venues. One of the funniest stories I can tell you happened after another night of partying. Teddy and I had gone out with about fifteen friends to all the different clubs the night before my big gig of the year. We ended up at a transvestite bar where they did drag shows called Backstreets.

It was a landmark in Atlanta. At about 5 am, I realized I had to be at the Talladega raceway at 8 am. We had been taking ecstasy, called Mollie, all day and night. At 3 am, my bright idea was I'd drive home to spray myself with some spray tan and maybe take another hit on the way there. Then I'll drive to Talladega straight from partying all night.

Ladies, if you're reading this and you have a boyfriend that would allow you to get in the car after not sleeping for 24 hours and then drive two hours in the dark alone high as crap probably not a great choice for a man. Where he knows hundreds of thousands of people will go crazy to meet you, you're probably with the wrong guy.

What a man's job is to protect you and even protect you from yourself? When you grow up without a Dad in the home or have a Dad that doesn't treat you with love, you don't even realize what's appropriate and how you should be protected.

I got to NASCAR, and my boss saw me, and he thought, "Oh my God," but he knew the stands were full of people and I would be far away because I would be sitting on the lead car going around the racetrack.

So I haven't slept in 24 hours in a red, white, and blue bathing suit higher than a kite about to sit on the lead pace car on the racetrack for NASCAR at Talladega. I heard, "OK, gentlemen! Approach your car." That was my queue to haul my butt up the ramp, get on the car, and go around the racetrack. The race track is not just a straight-away. It's a 45-degree angled track, so I'm basically leaning over, holding onto the hood of the car, waving at all the fans that are screaming show your tits over and over and over again.

I'm smiling, hanging on for dear life, waving while my eyes are rolling back in my head. Right about the time my butt hit the hood of that car, the second hit of E just kicked in. Everybody seemed so beautiful, and everything was magical. If they got a close-up of my face, it was probably super scary, teeth grinding, pupils huge wow. As the pace car finished its pace lap, we pulled over, and of course, I vomited everywhere. My boss took me up to the tower where no one could see me anymore, and I could watch the race until everybody left. He also wanted to make sure nobody saw how lit I was. I was there to sign autographs, but that didn't happen. Riding on the pace car; that was pretty awesome.

Yep, that's me in the above picture, and that's what I wore on the hood of that car. Sometimes NASCAR and things like that are launching pads for other exhibitionist-type jobs. Many girls and people that are molested go in different directions; some become lesbians, some become sluts, and some become exhibitionists. I became a free-spirited hippie exhibitionist.

There was a nightclub in Atlanta called 'The Cheetah,' which was the classy strip bar in town. This was a good idea. I can pay for the rest of my college by dancing. Girls, if you're with a guy that allows you to do such a thing to pay for stuff, then you're with the wrong man.

I was making really good money, and I never felt like I had to sell my soul to do anything that compromised my morals (like prostitution). Somehow, I justified stripping. I would come home with tons of cash, and my boyfriend and I would party or do something stupid with the cash. Some went towards college debt.

That lasted about a year and a half. I was always a good stripper. I would come home to my boyfriend every night, and I wouldn't drink too much at work, and I never set up business appointments with customers outside of work because I did not want to disrespect my man. How crazy is it that I was worried about disrespecting my man? Time went on, and our relationship became more and more toxic. One night we were out and had to take the train home. We had gotten into a huge argument, and he was acting crazy; I did not want him to come home because I was scared of him. I left him on the train and figured he would find a ride home. He was livid when he finally got home, and I knew things would go wrong.

The minute he entered the house, he started punching holes in the wall and throwing my things, including my TV, off the balcony. I called my Mom to come get me out of there, which she did. She pulled up in the apartment's parking lot, looking like she saw a ghost. She couldn't believe what she saw. I got in her car quickly, and we sped away. I called his parents to say you need to come get your kid. I'm going to call the cops. Your son needs rehab. They begged me not to call.

Part of the problem was that they always enabled their son, especially his Mom, which really didn't work out for him later in life, that's for sure.

He would also twist the truth, so I always felt unsure of what actually happened. Remember when I said the devil gets us off our path three ways? Well, this was pure deception all the way through. I didn't know how to see through things. I didn't trust myself enough to stand up for the truth and call BS. I knew the relationship was toxic but didn't know how to get out. I knew his parents were still married. That was the rock I built my foundation on, and somehow, in my mind, he and I could work it out. That Christmas, he came home with me to England, Arkansas for Christmas and proposed to me in front of my entire family. It was a beautiful thing. My family had Christmas at my Meme and Papas every year until I was thirty-five. I said yes, and the wedding plans began. Well, my Mom planned everything. She's super good at planning events!! My Mom and I planned the wedding, and it was beautiful. The church was right in the heart of Atlanta, right on Peachtree Rd. The church was an old Presbyterian church. The church was glorious, with three-story steeples and 30-foot-tall stained glass throughout. The front staircase was steep and palatial and looked like stairs to heaven.

Teddy and I had to do six weeks of counseling with the pastor before we married. In one of our sessions, he brought out an article about people who lived together before marriage. The article said that people that live together before they get married are ten times more likely to get divorced. I remember that pastor saying, "I'll marry you two, but you know the facts." I wasn't walking with God at all then, and I just thought he was old and behind the times. Looking back, boy, was he right. On the day of my wedding, when all the bridesmaids were getting their hair done at the salon, I got a phone call from the salon. Now this was before the internet and cell phones. This call was a miracle. A guy called me that I was super close to in

Cali. His name was Adam. He began to tell me that he kept my modeling pic in his Humvee all his tour of Iraq to give him hope for coming home. He said he was still over there but had to call me that day. We had not seen or talked in five years and lived across the world from each other. He called the only number he knew, my grandparents' phone. They told him where I was, and that's how he found me at the hair salon.

I remember the receptionist at the salon handing me the phone, and he said," Polly, what's going on with you? I had to call you today". I told him he was calling me on my wedding day! He told me about the picture he kept of me to give him hope and let me know my worth and value. He said," Polly, you're not supposed to marry this guy; this marriage will cause you so much pain." At this point, I was in deep. I loved Theodore, and we had almost three years together, and it SEEMED like the right thing to do. Wow, two warnings before I got married. PLEASE listen to signs around you because the universe will send you signs and warnings. Just be open to them and to make a change even at the last minute. Your heavenly Father wants to protect us. We need ears to hear; even though what was meant for evil can be turned for good, why do you need to go down a path that won't bring you joy? My two beautiful kids are my good out of that whole situation. We had six groomsmen and, six bridesmaids, an opera singer who sang Ava Maria. We had 150 guests, and our families were from all over the country. The bridesmaids wore the dress from Indecent Proposal with Demi Moore and held one single Cal Lily. The theme was black and white for everyone. It was perfect. My dress was a princess ball gown with a Tierra.

The minute they announced we were husband and wife to our guests, I whispered, "My god, you're high as a kite." He had been partying all day with his groomsmen in the other room, and he said, "Shut up Bitch, just smile for the picture." Those were our first married words, which should've been a clue for both of us. I wasn't a perfect angel, either. I'm sure I was mouthy and did things that weren't perfect, too, but I believed love could conquer all.

Everyone was at the reception, a gorgeous mansion on Peachtree. I had all my family there to celebrate, which diminished the drama because I was so happy to have all of us together.

After we married, we flew to Mexico, and I know I got pregnant on our wedding night because I was sick as a dog in Mexico. One of the nights on our honeymoon, I noticed all these girls were flirting with my husband, but I just felt sick, so I went to the room.

The next day I could feel people looking at me and whispering, and I went to find my disposable camera he left at the bar the night before. I wanted them because they were all the pictures we had taken on our honeymoon.

When we got back to Atlanta, I went to develop the film, and of course, there were naked pictures of the women on the camera roll. I was devastated. Now I'm married, and I believe he's already cheated on the honeymoon. This was the beginning of a giant roller coaster.

As I said, the devil loves to get you off your path. He will try to deceive you into believing a lie. My lie was that we would have a good shot if his parents were still married.

A Bible verse, John 15:7, says if you abide in me and my words abide in you, you'll ask what you desire, and it will be done for you." God's words had not abided in me since I was about seventeen years old when my Dad came back into my life and went to prison. I didn't even know how to really ask for what I needed. Your thoughts provide the fuel for your words, and your words provide the fuel for your world. I'll repeat it: your **thoughts** fuel your words, and your words fuel your world. My thoughts were always, 'Maybe this will work out. I hope I don't end up like my parents.' We have to declare into existence what we want, or we will get what falls in our lap.

Chapter 9

GOING BACK TO CALI CALI

At this point in my life, I certainly wasn't declaring anything into existence! I was just constantly putting out fires mainly that I created. I didn't know a life with peace yet. Theodore and I lived in that apartment, and I found out I was pregnant 2 weeks after we got home from our honeymoon. I got pregnant either in the carriage leaving our reception on Peachtree Street or in Playa Del Carmen, Mexico. We are not quite sure which one. I immediately stopped doing everything. I didn't want to go out with my friends anymore, drugs were out of the question, and I certainly wasn't drinking. I knew that this little life inside of me was the beginning of a change, and because of her, maybe my husband and I would have an actual chance.

I got a great job at a little design firm after I graduated college at a company called Creative Design. They were the design division for Cort Rental Furniture. Their main objective was to design the interiors of model homes. My degree was in design and business, so this was my dream job. I could sell what I believed in and design. They were wonderful all through my pregnancy, and they couldn't have been sweeter. Teddy was moving up in his real estate career, and he was now working for one of his good friends in commercial real estate. We were both making OK money without selling drugs or stripping go figure, lol. I was terrified that these "normal "girls at my new job would find out about my past. I was repeating a pattern again. When I was young, I was one way at school and another way at home. I wasn't ashamed I just didn't want that part of me to shine through and mess up my new beginning.

During my pregnancy, we had a few fights, that's for sure. It was very hard for all of our friends and my husband because I was the first one who was pregnant. We were the party couple. He was the King, and I was the Queen. He still wanted to do what he had always done, which was a party. He went to all the doctor visits with me, and he was super excited. We both were because we wanted something different, and we wanted a change.

I was at work one day at my dream job, and everybody kept looking at me funny. On my way to work, I went to the gas station to get some gas. As I was pumping gas in my car, all these trucks came by and were honking at me. I was about eight months pregnant. Now remember, I'm thinking in my brain, I still look like I did when I worked at The Cheetah. I'm pretty sure I did (NOT). By the end of the day, finally, one of the girls from our design company came up to me and said, "Do you realize why we've been looking at you all day?" I had no idea! I think my brain was still repairing itself. I had put my pregnancy panties on the outside of my dress omg! Well, there goes my strategy of if you look good on the outside, you must be perfect on the inside LOL.

When I was about two weeks late for my little girl coming into the world, I made a list of things that had to be completed before I could have my baby. There were 37 things on that crazy list. I always had a set of beliefs that I told myself. I called it my own personal ten Commandments. These are things that you live by, sort of like things that your parents say and that you hold true to them as the gospel for yourself.

One of my ten Commandments was cleanliness is next to Godliness. I made a list of 37 things I had to get done in the house before my little girl could come into the world. If you want to know what my number two thing was, here it is. This will make you feel better if you are pregnant and know you're not alone in your craziness. Number two on my list to buy topiaries to put on my fireplace so my mantle was framed perfectly. How crazy is that? Out of all the things I could obsess over, I wanted some freaking topiaries to put above my mantle before my daughter could come into the world. Wow, that sounds like I was a lunatic.

Our little girl was born, and Theodore wanted to name her Carmen because she was probably conceived in Playa Del Carmen. I also knew that she was my little angel. When I was on tour with the Grateful Dead, my name was Polly Angel.

Those are some of the happiest times of my life, so that's why I named my little girl middle name Angel. She literally saved my life! I turned away from everything that was destructive, and my entire focus was on being healthy for her. Her room was precious. I painted an ocean on the bottom of the walls and put little starfish all over the walls. Her bed were mermaids and dolphins with a white eyelet canopy. The whole room was completely perfect. Although I lived in Atlanta, I still missed the ocean desperately in California.

The day she came into the world, we had eaten eggplant Parmesan at one of the local Italian restaurants that claimed that if we ate, it would put me into labor. We had been going to classes for a birthing method called the Bradley method, which is all about breathing with your partner and natural childbirth. I wanted to give my baby girl the best shot at entering the world. My grandparents, my aunt and uncle, and all of my closest friends waited in the waiting room while I gave birth.

It was beautiful, and my mom got to be in the room, although she and Theodore had many fights during my pregnancy because he thought it wasn't appropriate for my mom to be there. I wasn't having it any other way. It's always been her and I, and this wasn't anything I was going to let her not be a part of. As I tried to keep my birth plan in place, an all-natural birth, something happened. I had gone through 42 hours of labor with no drugs but severe pain. My body was in distress, and I could not dilate, so they finally gave me Valium, which helped me a little bit. Then they said we're going to have to do an emergency C-section unless you dilate. I said, "Do whatever you can to make sure she's the safest." So they gave me an epidural which was not part of my birth plan at all! I immediately dilated to ten within six minutes, and she was coming. When I did that final push and she came out, Teddy just looked at me and said, "Don't worry about it."

He kind of looked horrified. I knew at that point I must've pooped right on the table. Ladies and gentlemen, if you read this and you're grossed out, you're just going to have to laugh. This is just a natural thing and happens to many women in childbirth, so be ready. I'm pretty sure that wasn't part of my fabulous birth plan, either. With one more push, she was here.

They took my little girl, and they put her on a table on the other side of the room. I said, "Carmen, I'm over here." I was lying there in my stirrups, wanting her to know I was in the room. My little girl lifted her little body up and looked over at me, and then they rushed her out of the room. That's who she still is, always caring about other people first. They started putting blankets on me because I was shivering all over, and they rushed everyone out of the room. My placenta was attached to the wall of my uterus, and I was hemorrhaging. They thought I might die.

While everyone was going to go see the baby, no one knew what was going on with me. Thank the Lord I was able to get some blood, and I was OK. So families, please be flexible when you are stuck on a birth plan it might not go that way at all!

We left the hospital the next day and went to our new place. I remember arriving at our house and being so worried about how I was going to get inside. I had a little rocking chair in our bedroom, and I did not leave that room for two weeks. They call it post-partum. I call it post-crazy. My mom would stay with me, but I just couldn't leave the room. there was something in my brain about leaving the room. So we loaded up, and we went and stayed with my mom for a couple of weeks so that I could have some help because hubby had to work every day, and so did my mom from her house.

Some things changed with my husband when I gave birth but not everything. We did not have sex the entire time I was pregnant with Carmen, and he was still partying. His job was getting better and better, and I knew I was going to have to return to work. I found a wonderful nanny right by my job where I could go and see my baby girl during my breaks, but it broke my heart to leave her. I just couldn't stand it. I wanted to be that Betty Crocker mom that my mom couldn't be because she had to work all the time because she had a deadbeat ex, aka. My Dad.

She didn't get any child support, so she couldn't be with me. At that point, he and I were saving up so we could buy our first house, and it was important for us both to work. After a few times of "late" work nights, I knew something was going on with my husband.

When Carmen was almost a year old, she was still nursing, and he didn't come home for almost 2 days. I was worried sick, and this was before cell phones. I couldn't find him. Then there was a knock on the door. There was a taxicab driver, and he had my husband because he found him in a parking lot face down, and he found his ID. He had vomited all over him. I rushed him into the house and knew to put him in the shower because he looked like he was going to need to go to the hospital.

As I took care of him, I started to go through his pockets to see if I could figure out where he had been because he was incoherent. My baby, luckily, was in the other room asleep, and she did not know any of this was going on. As I looked through his pockets, I kept finding more and more receipts. He had been at the local strip bar for the past two days on and off and spent $5000. That was all of our savings to buy a house. I was devastated. I told him unless he went into rehab and got his life together, we did not have a shot at marriage. He agreed, and he went into outpatient therapy, and I went to therapy. Things began to get a little better in our marriage, and we started to bond and get closer.

I knew that he probably had cheated on me. I had a new baby, and I didn't want to know. I wanted a together family. Hurts from the past cannot heal unless they are lanced. The infection has to be cleansed before healing can take place. When God heals you, we still have our past memories, but unless they are filed properly, you will get triggered when similar situations come up. My situation that was coming up was that I wasn't good enough, What was wrong with me that he would spend all that money and go behind my back? I know now it didn't have anything to do with me. If we yield all our hurts to Jesus and are completely honest with ourselves, then real healing and restoration can happen. We both weren't even close to being healed of our past hurts and defeats at this point in our inner journey. We merely scratched the surface of God's healing and the unpeeling of our hurts inside. God gives us a new perspective where we don't dwell on the event that devastated us. I was still harboring pain, and I couldn't believe I picked someone who was somewhat like my Dad. He wasn't nearly as bad, but there were some similarities. I wish I had been healed back then. His job was at a new company, not with his friend, and they paid for the rehab. He went back to work there for a few months, but he always felt funny, and he was embarrassed.

All of our friends were still partying, and I missed California desperately. I was now only having to work a few days a week, and on my off days, I would take my little girl on adventures. At this point, she was about 16 months old. One day we went to Chuck E. Cheese, and I left my diaper bag inside of Chuck E. Cheese.

I pulled up front in my little Jeep Cherokee. I had the air conditioning on full blast and pulled right into an upfront parking place. I literally walked in the door, and they handed me the diaper bag, and I left for literally 1 minute. By the time I got back to the car, which was less than one minute, my little girl was passed out in the seat even though the air conditioning was running. The heat coming through the window was so hot, and the humidity was so terrible that she couldn't stand it. I also just found out that we were pregnant again. I eventually lost that baby with a miscarriage. We weren't too devastated. I don't know why I wasn't sad, but I knew everything would be OK. I think that helped prompt us to our next step.

I knew at that point that I wanted to get out of the South, and I wanted to go back to California. That night Theodore and I sat home, and I said, "If our marriage is going to make it, we're going to have to get out of here. I think you would love California. I know your mom and dad will be sad because they're in Alabama. My mom is here, but hopefully, my mom will follow us if we go first."

A month later, he went to California. I stayed in Atlanta so I could send him money so that he could get on his feet. He found a job in San Diego, and that Thanksgiving in 1999, we packed up our budget truck and drove west. My mama kept my baby as we hit the road. That road trip was bonding. We were on a new adventure, and it was like the slate got wiped clean of all the drama that we had had. We were hopeful for our future. Our U-Haul truck even broke down in New Mexico, and we played mini golf and drank beer at a local pub to pass the time. We were a team again, I felt.

When we got to San Diego, we found a little one-bedroom apartment, and he immediately went to work. I found a good job, and my mom flew to California and brought our little girl. After a couple of nannies and every single time I would leave my baby, she would cry hysterically. I just couldn't stand it anymore. Three months after leaving her and not knowing anybody in California, I came home one day and said J, I just can't leave her anymore. I said let's sell my car. Let's do whatever it takes so that I can stay home. I want to be with our little girl. I don't want anyone to take care of her but us. He agreed, and a miracle happened. Put your family first, and God will take care of the rest. Teddy got a raise within the next couple of months of exactly how much I was bringing in, so we were doing better. God is good.

Things were looking up. He wasn't using drugs, we were still having arguments, but they weren't as terrible, and we were able to get a cute little house in Mira Mesa. We had a big backyard with a little pool and a swing set. I had an art easel and a little playhouse where we would play. I felt alone a lot because now I was a homemaker. As fun as my daughter was, I missed being in the working world. I was used to having my own money, and now I had to get an allowance that was hard and caused a lot of resentment in our marriage. Carmen slept in between us from the beginning. I'm sure that didn't help our sex life. Amazingly, we got pregnant again. I read the book, "The Family Bed." and that's where that idea came from. I also think I still hadn't healed that little 4-year-old inside of me, and I wasn't going to ever let anything like that happen to my baby girl.

I called my Mom in Atlanta and begged her to move. By the time I was 6 months pregnant, my Mom came and moved 15 minutes away. The day she pulled up, I felt complete again. I knew I could have my Mom to be with when all the stuff would happen with Theodore because I knew it was coming. Carmen and I would go to the beach and be with my mom all the time every day was a new adventure. Our little nap time was every day at 2 o'clock, and I would drive around my minivan until she would fall asleep in her little chair. I loved being a mom, and I loved being with her.

Being a wife was a different story. I knew from my Mom how to be a great Mom, but I never learned how to be a great wife. My husband would come home from work, and the house would be perfect. Carmen was ready for him, and I cooked a somewhat good dinner. When he got home from work, he usually would retreat to the garage to "get his head right." I resented that. I didn't really ever get a break. When I would go to the store, he would watch her as he would lose it because I was gone. My outings and breaks were when she was asleep, and by that time, I was exhausted. If you're a Mom, please remember you need your time to be better for everyone. That was hard on our marriage.

I decorated her room and had someone come out and custom-paint a beautiful mural on the wall. It was perfect. I had all of my dolls growing up on a little shelf, and she had her own trundle bed. Ted and I needed to get her out of our bed and into her own. That just didn't work. She wanted to be with us, and we were both just too tired to fight. In some weird way, it was our security because our marriage wasn't the best, but it wasn't the worst, and her being happy pacified the emptiness in our love life. On the weekends, we would go on family trips to the pumpkin patches or the zoo. She was my world. The pain I felt from the past hurts in our marriage I had not dealt with. I had a wall up to being truly vulnerable in my marriage.

Ted and I had lots of fights. I was really a nag about the house and being clean. I was at home a lot, and when he would come home, I just felt like the maid, not his sexy wife or appreciated in any way. I now know my self-esteem was super low. I had this underlying story going because I was an at-home mom, which must mean I must be a loser. I used to call at-home moms *meatloaf makers,* and now I was one. I'm sure my obsession with the kids was partially so that I didn't have to deal with our failing marriage. My pregnancy with baby Wesley was a good one. I did not have hardly any complications. Every day Carmen and I would play on the swings with the neighbors, or we would go on long walks, or we would go to her mommy and me group or whatever activity I had her in. Looking back, me being on the go so much, I think I was trying to prove I was better than just a meatloaf maker and that I was Super Mom.

When we have pain from childhood, especially not having a Dad, we struggle with identity. I struggled with feelings I needed to justify why I was home. I would overdo everything to prove I was good enough and ok to be at home. My mom had now started this organization, and for the past ten years, she was able to work from home. That's how she could just up and leave Atlanta. I had gone on many Vegas trips with her before I ever had kids. Her organization was the voice for third-party maintainers or computers. For example, if you wanted to get your computer fixed and you didn't want to go to Del, and you wanted a third party to fix it, she was a voice and had an organization for all those groups. Every year she would have an international conference in Vegas, and I was so lucky that I got to go. Carmen was two, and this year was particularly important because Theodore and I were already on the skids. I was exhausted from everything I had I would put into being a mom. I probably should've put more into being a wife, but I was just so angry with him for so many things. I was pregnant with Wesley, and the conference was in March, so I was 6 months pregnant. This year the conference was at Caesar's Palace. All day long, Carmen and I would play in the pool, and at night, we would meet my mom for dinner. Vegas had the best places to eat, and Carmen would love seeing all the excitement at dinner. One place even had an aquarium inside the restaurant right next to our table. This was such a blessing for me to be able to have this escape and show Carmen something so cool!

During the day, she and I would walk through the casino to go get ice cream and go to the pool. This was probably my favorite thing that I did every year with the kids, and for the next 20 years, we got to go with my Mom and Tagalong. She always got a penthouse or premier suite because she brought so many people there, and we were able to stay with her. Carmen was not potty trained yet. This is the first time she had ever seen a bidet. I wanted to potty train her before the new baby came, so this was my big chance. My brilliant idea was to train her on the bidet. She loved knowing the water would squirt the ceiling if no one was sitting on it. The minute she knew that she could sit on that little Benoit and her treat would be her being able to see that water squirt in the air if she went potty there, that was it. My little girl was potty trained at Caesar's Palace because of a bidet. I don't know any other little cute two-year-old that can say that. That was our last Mommy-daughter trip before Baby Wesley came into the world.

The day Wesley was coming into the world, our neighbor said they would watch her for us, and Ted and I went to the hospital. This was July 3rd, and Wesley was born 12 hours later. There weren't any complications, and he was born on July 4. Right after he was born, they whisked him away to the ICU because he had meconium in his lungs. Teddy wheeled me up to the top parking deck at the hospital to watch the fireworks. I needed to not worry about my baby. I knew that he was going to be a special baby too. I told him until he was eight that all the fireworks on July 4th were just for him. That wasn't a great idea in hindsight. My baby boy spent two weeks in a new tent to help his lungs work better, and every day, I would go and nurse him. This was so hard I felt so torn. After two weeks, he was well and finally got to come home. The entire time I was pregnant, hubby and I had not had sex at all. I had numerous phone calls from different people that he was having affairs with different women in the office, and I just couldn't prove it. We drove to Newport Beach after he was born to rekindle things. We were at a bar, and a girl hit on me. This was the first time my husband was interested in me in months. I was devastated that I wasn't enough for him. In my unhealed heart of not knowing my true identity, that is what I felt. Here I was with 2 small kids, and I was now a stay-at-home Mom, and I just felt stuck and devastated and mad all at once. I felt so hurt in my heart why would he need some extra stimulation from another woman? I didn't even try for any rekindling after that. I was gun shy, to say the least.

I just sucked it up, put my feelings deep inside, and was so happy being a Mom and having my precious Carmen and Wesley. We were the 3 musketeers. I took them on so many adventures. Now I had two little kids that I would put down for naps at 2 o'clock and try to get done whatever I could after we had gone on our fun excursions for the morning. Wesley's room was decorated perfectly too, and he had an animal print bed. I put safari animals all over his wall to make it as boyish as I could. He never slept in his bed, either. We just pushed a twin up to the king bed, and we just had one giant family bed. Our marriage wasn't really doing so great, but my love for those two kids and being so happy to have a family was greater than any longing for romantic love. Sometimes when you don't handle what's going on in your relationship and you let it fester inside, there becomes just too much water under the bridge. A marriage has to be nourished just like your kids need that. Neither one of us was really trying anymore. I learned at a young age how to put on a mask, and this time it was slowly coming off. Here is one of my favorite poems that sums up what happens inside when you don't deal with your trauma.

Please Hear What I am Not Saying

Don't be fooled by me

Don't be fooled by the fact that

I wear a mask, a 1;000 masks

that I'm afraid to take off

Pretending is an art that's second nature to me

but don't be fooled

for god's sake, don't be fooled

I gave you the impression that I'm secure

That all is sunny and unruffled with me,

within as well as without

That confidence is my name, and coolness is my game

that the water is calm, and I'm in command

and that I need no one

but don't believe me

My surface may seem smooth,

but my surface is my mask

every varying and every concealing

beneath lies no compliance

beneath lies confusion, fear, and aloneness,

but I hide this. I don't want anyone to know it.

I panic at the thought of my weakness

and fear of being exposed.

That's why I frantically create a mask

to hide behind a nonchalant sophisticated façade

to help me pretend

to shield me from the glance that knows

but such a glance is precisely my salvation

my only hope, and I know it

that is if it's followed by acceptance

if it's followed by love

it's the only thing that can liberate me for myself

from my own self built prison walls

from the barriers I said erect

it's the only thing that will assure me

of what I can't assure myself

that I'm really worth something

<u>Written by Charles C Finn</u>

This describes the struggle that goes on between the damaged image and the false image before you can get to the healed image. Remember, we all had an original image when God created us, but when things happen in our life that aren't right and cause pain, we think of ourselves as damaged, bad, or negative, and we don't really want people to get close. However, when we become completely healed, we pick the right people, and we address false narratives about ourselves. We take our masks off so we can be vulnerable and experience the world for real. You have to dig into which is the part of me that is writing this book. Getting to the core of it all just like you will sit down and write your story and realize that things that happened don't have to define you.

My prayer is you will pick a mate based on your healed self, not your falsely damaged self, so you don't have to go through the pain I went through in my first marriage. That you will have the discernment and wisdom to see patterns that won't serve the future that you were called to. Your true destiny is fulfillment and immense joy, and service to humankind. Life will happen, and sad and unpredicted pain will come, and even if things happen that aren't perfect, you will have the tools and love of Christ in your heart to know God has you! That you didn't pick a path that would bring you straight into more pain in your life. That is my true desire for you by reading this book.

Chapter 10

A HOUSE BUILT ON THE ROCK DOESN'T CRUMBLE

Now don't get me wrong, I loved my kid's Dad, I loved having a family, I loved having in-laws that love their son so much, and

I absolutely loved being able to create a family and have someone to share everything with. However, we didn't really start right which caused lots of problems from the beginning. After little Wesley came into the world things were even rockier. Then 911 happened and I got more and more entrenched into the kids and all their activities.

Ted got pushed more and more to the side and when he would come home I was just angry. He started coming home later and later and some nights I would be sitting at home and it would be 9 o'clock. My day looked like this. Wake up with both kids, nurse Wesley, try to keep Carmen occupied so she doesn't get jealous, go in and make them breakfast, watch Barney and the Teletubbies for a couple hours, clean the house, prepare all the snacks, do laundry and then it's only 9am. We basically lived at the San Diego zoo and wild animal park. My son loved Legos and we went there at least once a month, just us 3 and maybe 1 of Carmen's friends. I was all in as the fun Mom.

Carmen had a best friend that lived next door who had a speech impediment that I couldn't even understand half the time. She loved this little girl, and that was my entertainment. I would walk next door, and I would watch them swing in the backyard for hours, sometimes it was 95°. I would just sit with my colicky baby strapped to me like a koala because if I put him down, he would scream.

By 1 o'clock, I had it, I was already exhausted. I would come home, and I would lie down with both of them and try to get them both to go down for a nap. Sometimes I was successful, and sometimes, only Wesley would go to sleep. I quietly would turn the baby monitor on, and now it was Mommy and Daughter time. I had so much guilt that I had to pay so much attention to the baby, so instead of doing house chores or anything that had to do with myself, I would play with my daughter. We would play Barbies, or we would take off all of our clothes and run around the backyard and get in the pool and swim, which she thought was the greatest thing ever. I would watch her drive her Barbie Jeep around the neighborhood. We would have two hours of mommy-daughter time when those days would happen with him.

Then Wesley would wake up, and it was time to feed him again. Carmen would already be tired and cranky, and around 4 o'clock, it would be time to make dinner and get the house picked up so everything would be perfect when hubby got there. Sometimes we would venture out during the day, but that was only two or three days a week. It was wonderful, but at the same time, I lost myself. The nights when hubby would come home late, I was just exhausted. Some nights I would dress up in lingerie just to try to get his interest, and he just wasn't interested. I thought maybe it was because I was just too fat or too matronly or something, but it seemed like he just wasn't interested. I understand the plight of all Moms trying to juggle it all. Looking back, if I had had more balance and realized it was ok to drop the ball every once in a while, I might have been happier. That whole mindset if I look good enough or if everything LOOKS perfect on the outside, then I'm ok. True healing had certainly not happened yet!

I had a very handsome neighbor that lived next door. He was ten years younger than me, and he was my daily excitement. Carmen and I would play in the backyard, and I would hear his dog outside barking, and we would talk over the fence. I felt just like that skit on Seinfeld. Our entire relationship was over the fence for like 6 months. Oh, how I looked forward to him coming outside, and he would tell me how beautiful I was and how lucky my husband was.

I was starved for attention, and I just needed to look inside and realize I was beautiful to God always. He told me he would hear us yelling at each other at night all the time, and he was so sorry that there was so much abuse in the relationship.

Somehow I found him so endearing, and I felt justified in always being so upset with my marriage. I had no idea he had a crush on me. I was just happy I had someone to talk to. The months went by, and so did my hair color. That's always been my go-to to change my hair color one million times, and maybe that would make me feel better. I went platinum blonde from dark brown, hoping that would excite my husband to want me.

My neighbor always asked me to go do things, and I would tell my husband the neighbor thinks I'm cute, and he would just roll his eyes and say he just doesn't know you. I just wanted some response, like some attention is better than no attention. Needless to say, my self-esteem was shot. I knew my husband had been with many women because I had already received many phone calls. I just tried to blow them off. As many of us Moms think, if we just want to keep our little unit intact regardless of ourselves, sometimes we have to play dumb. I knew inside what was going on, and it was tearing me apart. That's not what God wants, and that is not how marriage was intended. It is a partnership, a love affair, a comforter, a best friend, and a lover. After many attempts, one night, my neighbor asked me if I'd like to go to have drinks with him. I was feeling particularly vulnerable that day. I told my husband around 6 o'clock, "The neighbor wants to take me out for drinks, so maybe I'll get lucky." Ha, ha. I was joking. I'll never forget what my husband said, he said, "Well, you better grease yourself up like the big fat pig that you are, and just maybe, if you get him drunk enough, he will want to screw you because I sure don't."

We hadn't had sex in over a year at this point, and Wesley was 1-year-old. That was my tipping point;

everything I knew inside went right out the window. So that's what I did all 31 years of me. I greased myself up like the fat pig that I felt like I was and went over to our neighbor's house. We went out drinking in a young part of town, and I felt alive again, I felt pretty again. By about the fourth margarita, I felt horny again too. WOW! That night I had sex with my neighbor in the parking lot of the bar, in the alley of the next bar, and then in his car on the way home. I remember the awkward drive home with him, wondering what we had just done. I know tequila can make your clothes fall off but crap! I looked over at his sweet 22-year-old face, he was smiling ear to ear, and he asked me if I would be ok? I was happy, and mad and sad and disappointed in myself all at once. Part of me felt the feeling of revenge, and part of me felt fear of losing my family. I was all over the place. My Meme always used to say two wrongs don't make a right. I really wasn't in church and didn't really feel bad about anything. I kind of felt like my husband had it coming.

My neighbor thought I was going to leave my husband for him, and so the talks over the fence became very awkward. He got deployed and asked me if I could watch the dogs for the next three months, so I did. That was my getaway. I would go over to his house and stay there without him being there since it was right next door and take care of his dogs and enjoy my time away from the house because it was so uncomfortable. When he returned, Ted and I had somewhat patched things up even though I had not told him my dirty secret. Our house was already built on sand, and now I could feel everything crumbling. Teddy was doing better at work and at home. My kids were healthy. I knew I wasn't going to do that anymore, and I just had to keep my mouth shut.

See, the devil is a liar, and he tells you that keeping a lie to yourself will just make everything OK, but all it does is tear you up on the inside. It is essential that you become extremely vigilant about what enters your mind daily, what you hear affects how you think and what you believe. The prophet Isaiah had insight into how important it is to fill your ears with words that will produce joy. Eventually, if you hear something enough over time, you form a belief, and that belief will produce a corresponding action. All I could hear was what a nag I was, what an angry woman I was, how I wasn't really attractive anymore, and nobody would really want me so I better just suck it up. If you let those negative thoughts take over your mind, it will lead to a destructive act, usually a self-sabotaging act like what I did. If you get anything out of this book, be mindful of your thoughts. Remember, thoughts cause actions, so let what goes in your ear and what you see, and what comes out of your mouth be positive so that you can have a life that you deserve to have. Your very thoughts are powerful, and your words can change the course of your destiny.

If someone in your life is constantly putting you down, you need to get away from them. If it's a marriage, get some counseling, go in another room, and don't listen to it. Turn your phone on some positive music, and talk to a friend that always makes you feel better. Don't focus on those negative words, and don't repeat them to justify your sadness; it only hurts your soul more. After my neighbor came back from his deployment, he asked me what I was going to do. I said, "I'm going to stay with my husband, that's the right thing to do." So he moved, and that was the end of that.

My husband was starting to make a whole lot more money, and he got a new car. I just put all of that craziness out of my mind. You might think getting new things, going places, and filling your time will erase your memory, but it just puts it in a not-so-healthy file in your mind, trust me!

I still had my minivan, and we put our name on a list in an up-and-coming new suburban neighborhood called 4S Ranch. This was where all the people that were starting to make money were moving to raise their children because it had a great school district and wonderful parks. This was it. I felt like I arrived and I was finally going to have our dream home. I made the salespeople in the new home's office brownies and went to visit with the kids every day so we could get into one of the first phases. This is when the real estate market was so hot in 2002 before the collapse in 2006. Believe it or not, we made it into phase 2 pricing. We were ecstatic, we got the house for about $450,000 it was 2800 square ft. with four bedrooms and three baths. Trust me, that is a deal in Southern California. A tiny little backyard where we could have a swing set. I knew there were going to be families that I could relate to and hang out with all the time. I was over the moon for our new life.

Now it was moving day, and Theodore had to work. I had to figure out how to balance having my little boy with the move. I had found a sweet lady who would keep Wesley because he was little. My Mom took Carmen for a few days before the move so I could move without having to handle her too. After a day with the movers, I went to pick up my baby boy. I put him in his little car seat and drove back over to the old house so that I could steam-clean the carpet. We needed to get our deposit back, we were still struggling a little financially, and we needed that 2500 bucks for lots of things. As I was driving over there, Theodore was following me. He had been drinking tequila at work. He thought that I had stolen his wallet. He was driving right on my bumper and flashing his lights. I knew something was wrong, and I had not seen him all day. I had zero help during the move. I finally pulled over, and when we got out in some random person's front yard, he started screaming these gross names at me. We had about 8 months since the incident with the neighbor. Things were still bad at home, and our sex life was still nothing. I had just received a phone call a few weeks before from the very woman from his office who threw my baby shower for Wesley.

She told me that she was sleeping with my husband, I confronted him about it then, and he lied, of course. All that was in my head so I took a swing at him, and he hit me right in the face. I had a slight black eye. I was crying hysterically as I was sweeping the floors at the old house, trying to get our deposit back. I felt hopeless even though we were about to move into our dream home. He didn't help clean at all he left and told me it was all on me since he made the money and I was just the paid help. I remember my back killing me, but I just had to press on. I had my little boy in his little car seat with me at that house. I would cry and look across the room at his sweet little face, and suddenly my pain and heartache would leave. I was so happy Carmen wasn't there because she would have witnessed all of this.

After everything was clean and I had moved all day, like a 15-hour day, I went to our new home all by myself and put Wesley in the bed next to me. I laid down without my husband there. Then in the middle of the night, he came into the bedroom and slapped me on the face while I was nursing the baby. He told me how crazy I was and how I twisted everything that had happened like it was all my fault. I didn't really fight back because somehow I thought I deserved all this, that somehow it would be OK for him to treat me like that since what I did almost a year ago. Although he didn't know, I just felt like he could treat me like that. When we don't deal with the truth, and we constantly bury our feelings, we let the devil enter our minds and truly twist how we see things.

The next day when my Mom flew back to San Diego to see our new house and bring Carmen for the first time, she knew something was wrong. I had a white stripe going through one of my eyebrows. I was literally eating myself up inside with all the pain that I had been thinking that I deserved from him to treat me like that. I just swallowed it and put the mask on like I knew to do oh so well. I learned that at an early age. I had not filed anything properly from my past. When you file your past traumas where they belong, in the past, you'll never accept behavior like that from anyone, regardless of what you've done.

NOBODY ever has a right to call you names or to treat you in any way but with respect. NOBODY certainly ever has the right to put their hands on you. I wanted this happy new life. I had my dream home, my new puppy, and a together family, which was always my dream. I just grinned and bared it, and I did not tell my Mom what happened, but she knew like Mommas always do.

Our happy little family wasn't really so happy. This was our first Christmas, and I was so happy to decorate our yard with Wesley's favorite thing, a Choo-Choo Carmen. I always wanted to be the best decorated house, and we were. Never judge a book by its cover. You might think your friend or neighbor has a perfect life. You don't know until you know.

So now my life is filled with stuff to occupy the pain inside. We were moving on up. I was going to have the house that I dreamed of and have a little family in the burbs. I knew things were going to start looking up. I just focused on decorating our home beautifully because I knew being busy would keep my mind off the pain. We had the Tommy Bahama palm tree wallpaper. I had custom blinds and beautiful window coverings made for every room. I had Carmen's room painted with fairies. I had our room decorated with Tommy Bahama fans and a tropical theme that looked like an oasis. I had picked out flawless pillow shams. Our carpet was Berber, and it was gorgeous. I was so excited for our new life. We had our backyard hand-stamped, and we had a little puppy named Rosie. Everything was coming together. I had two kids and a husband. I could stay home in a neighborhood that my kids could enjoy and love. I just immersed myself in the neighborhood.

I didn't have Jesus in my life yet, so I just filled my life with shallow things to cover up the hole I had in my heart. Carmen was starting at the brand new school in the neighborhood that all the neighbors went to we could even walk to.

There were tons of burb kids for my kids to play with. I joined the local bunco group, which was a group of ladies that, once a month, would get together and have the best time. Basically, we called it "Drunkoh". We would just play dice games, and someone would win 20 bucks at the end of the night, and we thought it was amazing. Every day was filled with different activities for the kids. Carmen was in karate 3 days a week for an hour and a half, and Wesley and I would walk around with all the other moms and try to figure out something fun to do. What usually meant jumping in the fountains and playing at Starbucks.

When hubby would come home at night, we would usually argue, and I would make dinner, and we would sit as a family. He was a good Dad when he came home, he would play with the kids out in the yard and give me a break.

I was learning how to have some balance since Wesley was two, and he was a little bit better. The suburban life went on for a couple of years, where we would go to parties with the neighbors and have a good time and put on our masks like most of the people in the burbs. If it looks good on the outside, everything must be perfect. I was on the PTA, and I joined Girl Scouts with Carmen and was one of the co-leaders. I was on duty most of the time, even when he was home. Every Girl Scout meeting we ever had, Wes went he loved being the tagalong little brother. Finally, I was able to be the Mom I dreamed of. Being able to volunteer at both kid's schools made it all worth it

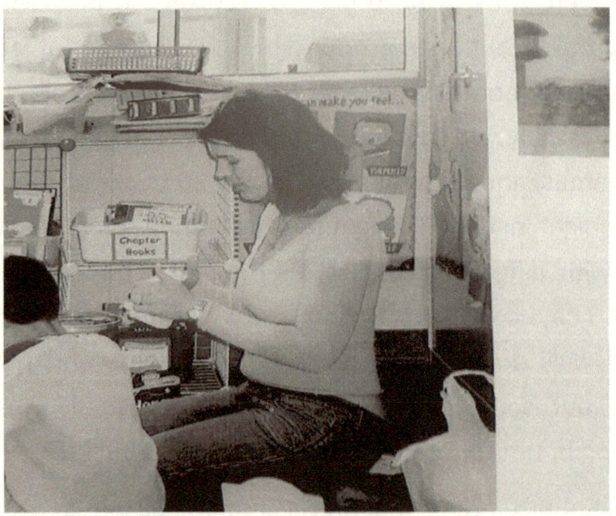

This is me volunteering at Wesley's sweet little preschool.

I knew it was time to return to church because I had a secret inside myself that was just killing me. Theodore and I were really on the skids because I was just so unhappy with him and so many things that he would say to me that just hurt. Even when we would go on family trips like Disneyland and train rides, I was always naggy. I just couldn't get out of the "poor me" syndrome. I'm sure that was a big part of our distance. You can't control other people, but you can control your actions and attitude. I felt like I deserved it and like I had a scarlet letter on my chest that, deep down, I would allow him to say things to me. All the stuff filling our time never took away the scars we both had inside, especially me.

One night we got into one of the worst arguments we had ever gotten into. It was almost ominous that both kids went to sleep early, which was unusual. We had drifted far apart, so when we had a time when we should be bonding and getting closer, there was just awkward silence. I wasn't perfect by any accord, and I would definitely egg it on. I would bitch and nag about little things. I look back and think most of this was about negative attention which at the time I felt was better than no attention. What I really wanted was to be desired as a woman and have a marriage that was joyful. If you hear yourself in my words, take a step back and ask yourself what it is you really want. It's not him picking up the towel, it's usually way deeper than that.

This night wasn't anything like either of us wanted. He had been drinking, and our yelling escalated to where I could barely contain my rage. I am not justifying anger in any way, but I was holding it all in, and I went to kick him. He grabbed me and threw me up against the wall, held me by the throat, and told me he would kill me if I ever did that again. That was it, and I knew I was going to leave. I went to Starbucks the next day and I had bruises on my arms and on my neck. The sheriff was there and asked me what happened.

I told the officer, so he filed a report and said that my husband needed to go to anger management classes. I didn't feel like I was really a victim because I was kind of tough now. I had gotten a personal trainer and was working out a ton. I was truly building that hard shell on the outside. I'm sure it was to guard my heart that was shattered inside. I felt like somehow this wasn't really all happening, but it really was. I knew what I was doing wasn't working for either of us, and the only answer I knew was God. I couldn't change him or the past, but I could change how I reacted to him. My whole life, I had been in church, and ever since I walked away from God, it was like my life just kind of spiraled. I wanted my kids to start going to church, so we started going to a local church around the corner. I knew I needed to go to therapy for myself and the couple's therapy to try and salvage our crumbling marriage.

I kept hearing the word abundance, abundance, I should have abundance. That still voice I had heard as a young girl kept hearing it say this to my soul. I kept thinking I have a beautiful house, I get to stay home with my kids, my daughter is in karate and Girl Scouts, I'm on the PTA, and I'm super involved in the neighborhood. I get to play with my little boy, buy him any toy he wants, and take him everywhere with me. I had an abundance of things to do, and all the material things I THOUGHT would make me happy, but I didn't have an abundant life. What I knew was missing had nothing to do with materialism or consumerism. What I was talking about is the fact that it is God's will for us to live a life without lack. I was missing true joy and peace inside. He will provide us with every possible thing that we need to be successfully fulfilled in our purpose, and that will maximize our potential for us to have spirit-inspired thoughts, declarations, and conversations, divinely appointed relationships, and true fulfillment and joy. I didn't have any of that, just hollow moments filled with short intervals of joy with my kids. I dare you to start making a masterpiece out of your life, not a master disaster which is what mine has become.

I started going to see this therapist at church. She gave me the Bible that I have today, and I started to read it again, and the words just started jumping out at me. So one day I told her about my dirty little secret that I did almost 2 years ago with the neighbor. She began to tell me the story about the wise and the foolish builder in Matthew chapter 7 it says, everyone who hears My words and puts them into practice is like a wise man who builds his house on the rock. The rain will come down, the streams will rise, and the wind will blow and beat against the house, yet it will not fall because it is built on a solid foundation. However, everyone who hears these words and listens to God and does not put them into practice is a foolish man who builds his house on the sand. When the rain comes, the streams rise, and the wind blows and beats against that house, and it falls in a great crash. I knew exactly what this meant, and it could not have been more obvious. My house was built on the sand. So many lies between the two of us that we had never talked about. Especially my event with the neighbor that I had kept a secret. Then there was my constant nagging of him and me not trusting anything he did. Our house was completely built on a lie, and that's why it was so shaky all the time.

I knew at that point I had to tell my husband the truth regardless that he had never told me of all the affairs that he had. Even though I had gotten many phone calls from different women. Even at his job, including the woman that threw a baby shower for my son. Even she was having sex with my husband at work. It wasn't up to him to tell me any of those things, but it was my job to tell him the truth. I needed confirmation. I'm telling you this because maybe in your life, there's something you need to tell someone, and instead of just blurting it out, you need to get confirmation that it is the right thing to do for you. God will show up in some mysterious way to let you know that's what you need to do.

This particular day I picked up my son from his cute Christian preschool. Wesley had his cute little policeman uniform on. He always dressed up in some new costume every day. He was adorable. He had a speech impediment when he was born, and he couldn't say his R's, W's very well or his Al's, but I could understand everything he said. I understood his little language, and I took him to speech class three times a week for an hour each day all the way across town. Then I would take him with his little organic snacks to his preschool for two hours before I picked Carmen up from first grade, then go back and pick him up.

This particular day after I had decided I was going to tell Teddy everything, I needed real confirmation. I was so afraid of the outcome. Wesley got into the car, and for the first time in his whole life, he spoke so clearly, he said, "Mama is our house built on the rock or on the sand?"

I was literally just in counseling, and she had just asked me that question. Could I ask for more confirmation? There was no way that my little boy would've known this because he was in his class. He handed me a little bag of sand, and I just started to weep in the car. As I sat in the car, I knew God was either going to restore my marriage or I was going to have to face the consequences of what was next.

I went home that evening, and after I tucked the children into bed, I went downstairs. I told my husband everything! I told him that I had seen (the neighbor) two times. The first time was the night he told me to dress up like a fat pig, and maybe if he was drunk enough, he might want to screw me. That was the first night I had been unfaithful to my marriage. There was one more time that I was unfaithful. I did that a year after my neighbor moved. I went to see if I wanted to be with him because my marriage was in such shambles. I thought maybe he and I should be together.

I borrowed my in-law's car and lied to them about who I was going to see. He was now stationed an hour from their home in the south. This was 3000 miles from San Diego. I slept with him one more time. After that night, I knew that this young man needed to have a life of his own. That he would be taking on two kids that weren't his, and that it would be drama for his young life, and it was time for me to walk away. I thought my marriage could be repaired if I just kept my secret. It literally was eating me up inside.

That night as I sat on our imported leather designer sofa in our perfectly furnished home, I told my husband everything, and he was just in shock. Things got super violent, and I felt like I deserved all of it. He did not hit me this time. However, the things he called me were worse than physical abuse, and I just felt like I completely deserved all of it. I started going to Sunday school every Sunday and taking the kids to church. Theodore would come sometimes when he didn't have to work. He was now working downtown rebuilding downtown San Diego in a high-rise condominium complex. He had gotten yet another promotion and was a marketing director. Slowly we were drifting even further.

Our marriage really started to crumble even more as we started going to therapy. I remember telling the therapist what happened with the neighbor and crying so hard about the shame and guilt I felt. I'll never forget her looking up from her notepad with her glasses on the bridge of her nose, and she said, "Well, if you're not going to butter her bread, somebody else is. What's wrong with you? I'm sure you've been getting your bread and butter a lot and not from your wife. You are a lucky man that you have a wife who wants an honest and real relationship." I was so relieved a little inside from getting some validation from her. Needless to say, he never wanted to go back.

I knew at this point that I had given my power, authority, and dominion to the father of lies. I had allowed condemnation, shame, and bitterness to take root in my heart. I wanted to get in the right standing with God. I knew that this fight for our marriage could not be won by therapy alone but by getting on my hands and knees in prayer.

One night after telling my husband everything, I was washing the clothes upstairs. I was so upset I left the sink turned on upstairs. We all went to the store for a few hours, and when we came home, the entire house was flooded. We both were in shock and thought, 'Wow, just one more nail in the coffin.' I also thought maybe this is God washing our sins away and our past so we could have a clean slate in our marriage.

Our insurance company put us up at a hotel for the next three months, which was wonderful. Ted came into some money at work, and we were finally starting to get along. We had to stay at a Residence Inn, so it was like a small condo. This place had nightly luaus with free food, so I didn't have to stress about dinner, a great pool, and the best part was the daily maid service. I was really thinking that God had washed away everything and that we were going to be OK.

I really wanted a Mommy makeover, so I got a brow lift, some liposuction, and my lips tattooed, so I could look and feel like a woman again instead of just a Mom. He was super sweet to me for the next 2 weeks. Wasn't I so pretty???

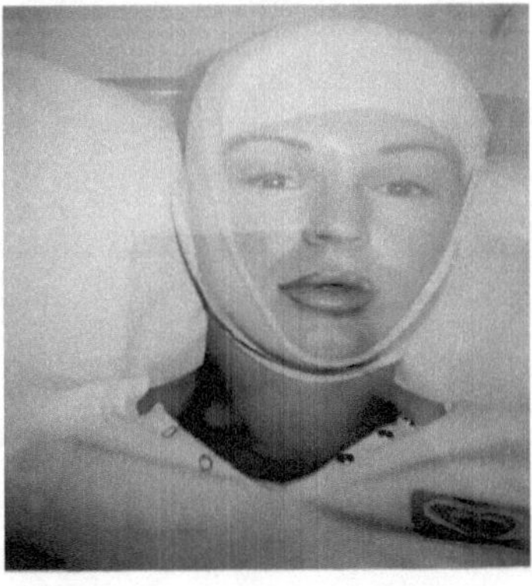

Life was starting to look up. When we would go to the luaus at our hotel, Carmen would get dressed up, and we would go and have a ball as a family. Dancing to Hawaiian music with my entire family smiling, it felt like my dream. It seemed like our family was coming back together and that it was being built on the rock this time. I called that 3 months our honeymoon phase part 2. After three months, we moved back home. I think that the memories in that home were still built up inside. There was still major tension right when we moved back. I didn't really get how to fight in prayer for my marriage. I hadn't really dealt with all my childhood pain. That pain not dealt with is what manifested my current pain and heartache and my situation.

I put my energy into feeling better about myself, not just being the perfect Mom. I started going to the gym, which was a huge release. He bought a new Porsche, and we had a Range Rover he was working on later and later every night again. I was getting fitter and fitter physically and spiritually. The more fit I got, the more I wasn't happy with the status quo because I realized I deserved more, and so did he. We started going on date nights which was somewhat awkward, but we were trying. The kids were still in all their activities, and I was trying to be a super mom and super wife all at the same time and super Christian everything. I was doing life based on performance, not based on just being.

One Saturday night, we went out on a date. I wore a new black dress that showed off my new curves and body, and I felt like we were really on a date as a newlywed couple. I was excited for a fresh start. We went to his company work party. There was this older gentleman who was about 70. He asked me to go downstairs at the party to get a tape out of his car. Ted was busy trying to have conversations with all the different work partners that he had. It wasn't the best date night romantic adventure, but at least we were out of the house together without the kids. I went downstairs with the guy and got the tape. When I came back upstairs, Teddy looked at me like I cheated again. This man was literally 75 years old, and I was 34 at this point.

After he got through schmoozing all his business partners, and I had a few glasses of wine and had meaningless conversations with strangers, we left. On the way home, my husband was a little buzzed more than me. My 2 glasses of wine over the course of 4 hours were fine. I drove us home that night. As I was driving home with both kids in their car seats in the back, I thought they were asleep. We picked them up from my mom's house after we got through with our date. I figured as soon as the car got rolling, they would pass out. As soon as he thought they were asleep in the car, he immediately started calling me various names and accusing me of being a cheating whore the entire drive home.

The name-calling just kept getting worse and worse, and I just was getting sicker and sicker of it all. I had apologized profusely for the past, and I thought we were over the hump.

That night it was like a light went off. I knew he would hold that 1 thing over my head forever, even after our 3-month honeymoon at the hotel. We pulled into the driveway, and I took Carmen out of her car seat to put her on the bed. She had heard everything that was said the whole 20-minute drive home. She wasn't asleep at all. She looked up at me with her precious little brown eyes and asked me a very important question. She said, "Mommy, what is a F-ng whore, and why does dad always call you that?"

That was it. I knew that my life would be full of taking Xanax or whatever I could take to stay in this marriage and be numb. I knew that my daughter would watch me try to be a super mom, and her dad would probably always come home and call me names, I would fight back and that we would be in this toxic cycle forever if I didn't do something. That night I cried myself to sleep and held both kids in the bed. Ted fell asleep on the sofa or in the guest bedroom. I don't know where. The next day I called my mother to come get the kids for the night, and I called an attorney. I put his stuff out in the front yard and changed the locks. That was it. I filed for divorce that very day and that was the beginning of our next chapter. The enemy comes to steal, kill, and destroy, but God comes to give life and life more abundantly, and that certainly is not what I was having.

Chapter 11

THE DIVORCE AND CUSTODY

There's nothing that the devil hates more than marriage because marriage symbolizes how God loves the church and unity and he hates that. Divide and conquer is the devil's playbook. If there's only you, it's a lot easier to get attacked. When a seal swims alone in the sea they have a 90% chance of getting eaten by a predator. Like it says in the word, "Where two or more are gathered, there I'll be also."

I filed for divorce that year, 2004, right before Christmas and right after my 35th birthday. I had a trainer at 24-hour fitness that helped me find my inner and outer strength again.

I had gotten down to a nice size, and I felt better about myself physically. I watched that movie with Jennifer Lopez where she was in a relationship, and the guy was abusive, so she had become tough. That's what I did. I put my big girl panties on, and I trained hard. Sometimes you put on that outer tough shell to hide the pain that you have inside. I decided to go to a mediator in San Diego. I knew that we could agree on a lot of things in the divorce as far as finances and custody. I wanted child support for both kids. We would switch every other holiday and birthday we would celebrate together, and he would give me spousal support, I hoped.

My dream from the time I gave birth was to be there for everything for my kids and I did not want that to change because of the divorce and neither did he. After going back-and-forth to court many times we decided we would sell the home and that we would split the equity. The housing market from 2002 until 2004 skyrocketed in San Diego. I figured I would have plenty of money to survive after we split up everything.

That Halloween we were separated. He was staying in a little condo downtown and we were about 30 minutes away. I didn't want him to not be with us on Halloween since that was such a fun time for our family, so he came up to be there for trick or treat. I will never forget how our family got dressed up like a family as if we were normal and everything was just peachy. I gave him a costume that looked like a big giant fat baby. I thought that was pretty fitting and he filled his baby bottle with vodka. Let's just say that night didn't go like one big happy family event and the next day he left.

That was the beginning of me really not having any boundaries at all because I still hadn't forgiven myself fully. I had hoped that we could still be a together family but be divorced. My lack of self-respect and self-worth all in the name of trying to keep everything somewhat nor- mal for the kids actually cost me in the end. All the holidays we tried to pretend like we were still sort of a family.

That Christmas, we tried to celebrate like a family like we

always had. I remember him sleeping downstairs on Christmas Eve after we built all the kids' toys the night before. I felt so much guilt for not letting him come in our bed. I just couldn't go back there because the pain was too great. He begged me that night to put our family back together. I felt like such a bad person, but I couldn't let my wall down again, and I cried myself to sleep. I just knew I had already put the wheels in motion, and nothing except words had really changed with him. He was still the same as he was before I filed for divorce,

The next morning, we got up and our dog Rosie had just had pup- pies. Here it is Christmas morning and we had a divorce going on, living in a house we didn't know we were going to keep, both kids didn't really get what was going on because dad was still there, and now I had a house full of puppies. I just felt so lost but somehow I knew I was going to be OK.

In the middle of the storm, you can still have peace if you know where to turn. I hadn't forgiven myself fully yet. Forgiveness has an order. We have to get right with God before we can get right with others. I was learning to forgive him and me, but I had so much bitterness that was truly stifling my heart, and I wasn't free yet.

The time came to sell the house and we sold it for $710,000. I did not understand escrow or any of those things and I had allowed my husband to pay all the bills and control all the money. Looking back, I should've had my hands in the finances so that we could work as a team.

It was more like I was the babysitter and the maid and he was the bank. When we finally closed escrow I was ecstatic. I was so excited for my new life I thought I would have $150,000. The kids and I had gone to a new home development and put down a deposit on a brand new townhome. We wrote our names in the cement because we were so excited that we were going to have a new home.

It had been 5 months since we started the divorce process and now it was time to fly free or so I thought. I'll never forget the day when I went to the escrow office and the woman handed me the paperwork. I was waiting on a check and then came the biggest blow of all. There was no money left. Every single penny of our equity we had in the home was gone and I had no idea. I walked away with $10,000 and a beat up minivan. I was devastated! I couldn't believe that this was happening. As I stood with my crappy minivan in the title company's parking lot, I just cried in my car for an hour. I just felt so stupid and defeated.

I had to go over to the townhouse that I had put down the deposit at and beg for my money back. That was the beginning of me feeling so powerless and feeling like I was a nobody. When Satan comes in and strikes the hardest it's when you're at your lowest. It's when you're weak. He is the father of lies.

All I could think is I'm a loser, I'm stupid, I'm a nobody. That weighed heavily on me for years. I made that my identity was a loser single Mom in the burbs. I didn't really know yet how far I could depend on God. All I knew was to depend on having a good time and my looks. He gave up on me and prayed that the money that he was giving me every month would show up. That came with a price every month when he would give me the money, and particular words would be spoken that would solidify that powerless little girl inside and repeat in my mind what a loser I was.

Somehow I thought that was okay because at least I had money coming in. After all, I ruined our family. That's how I felt. All those feelings when I was 6 and my Dad killed himself, and I was powerless they were all still there. I'll never forget after the home sold, and the kids and I found this little three-bedroom condo right around the corner from their school with ugly blue carpet. I felt safe there. It was just the three of us, and they each had their own room, and we had a little garage that I could keep all their toys in. I had a solid $10,000 that I spent on some furniture. We had enough to get some cool groceries and now I was completely dependent on my ex-husband who was so angry with me. I had literally put myself in a position of being powerless. A repeat of my childhood. It's funny how we do that and we aren't even conscious of it when we are in the middle of it all.

I had my kids in all kinds of sports. Wesley played indoor soccer. At every game that I went to I was alone with Carmen. My ex, their Dad rarely came, so I felt free finally. I knew how to have fun and that would keep me from thinking about all the shame and guilt I had from getting divorced.

Every game I would see the hunkiest guy across the Soccer field and every week we would stare at each other. I finally got enough guts to put a note on his car for him to call me. Now I'm a southern girl at heart and I don't believe in making the first move but I was just ready to have fun and finally meet someone and have a good time. I put a big note on his lifted Chevy with my number telling him how cute I thought he was. Guess what? He called the next day. He was fun and hot and had a son my son's age. I felt connected. I met him at Christ- mas and in January Theodore had his family come out.

That January I went to meet the in-laws at a hotel and this new guy Dustin told me if you have the opportunity to put your family back together then that's what you need to do.

I was so confused because I was actually finally feeling peaceful and happy and I didn't want that roller coaster anymore. When I saw their dad and the kids being so happy playing with their grandparents I thought what have I done? Again I asked God for another sign, should I put my family back together? I wondered, as I stared at my kids play- ing in the pool with their DAD did he learn his lesson?

When Ted and I started talking that night I could tell nothing had changed. I felt like that was a sign that he was still pointing fingers at me and hadn't done any work on himself or admitted to anything.

If he would've been sober and asked me in a different way and suggested counseling and church, I believe that that night would've been pivotal and I might've just done it. However, that's like saying you're going to go on a diet and you go out and eat cheeseburgers all the time and think that you're going to lose weight.

Marriage requires real effort and marriage is also a lot of work. You can't always have the benefits from something when you're not willing to put in the true work that it takes. He hadn't done any work, he just started making more money and he was all talk. Talk is cheap. actions I can work with. Needless to say I didn't go back to him.

Every other weekend for almost 2 years when I would not have the kids that was my fun time to cut loose. Dustin and I went everywhere we went rock climbing, we went hiking, we loved to go to clubs and dance, we watched football and UFC we even played on a competitive coed softball team together, and yes, for the first time in years I finally felt like a sexy woman. I was not walking with the Lord, I was just kind of fake going to church. I guess you could say I was in my prime. He was a bodybuilder, blonde hair, blue eyes, and looked like an Adonis. After years of being with a man who didn't want me sexually I felt so good about myself with Dustin. He made me feel sexy again.

One weekend in particular, I guess I got drunker than normal, and he dropped me off because he was mad. I walked over to my little condo to the Hot tub and sat there alone. Then all of a sudden two guys walked in with

McDonald's French fries. I just reached over into their bag and ate every single one of their French fries.

I didn't even tell them my name and I didn't even talk to them. I literally just ate their French fries and got up out of the pool and left. God sends us people in the strangest ways. That man Tony has been one of my best friends now for 16 years and stood by my side through all my crazy condo days. When I wouldn't hang out with Dustin on the weekends, Tony and I had a crew and we would all go downtown. I called it the Asian flavor +2 Whiteys LOL. We would go to clubs and dance and have a ball. I was reliving my pre kid's days and loving it. The kids were doing well. I was working at LA Fitness part time so I could still pick up the kids from school. I would pick Wes up and take him to a little daycare for three hours so I could still work. The scheduling with my son was hectic but it was OK and we were doing good.

I was driving my Dodge Durango with a 7-inch lift kit and 22's on it, and I thought I was the cool Mom. If you're reading this and your suburban mom and you're divorced I understand your plight! Women always think that you're in love with their husbands or somehow that you want what they have. I found myself never even speaking to the men without their wives there because I didn't want anyone to get the wrong idea of what kind of woman I was. I just wanted to be happy and be in a safe place with my kids.

I was active at their schools and we had started going to a little church called city church every Sunday. When I would go I would sit in the back row and halfway hold my hands up because I had so much guilt inside about what kind of life I was really living. Every other weekend when the kids weren't around I was a sex freak, alcohol wasted, drugs every once in a while party girl.

However, those pastors loved my kids so much they would come and get them and take them places all the time. God was in the boat with me the whole time, and I just was too blind to see. They would pay for them to go to vacation Bible school. My daughter was in a really cool connect group, so she could connect with other girls. I had a community around me I didn't even really realize it as much then, but I sure do now. God was always watching after us. That's what a good Dad Does He watches over you and never stops loving you even when you mess up. I didn't realize that then.

When LA Fitness finally opened, we took a limo out partying, and I just felt like a rock star. I was sort of an outcast in our little rich suburban neighborhood, so having this gym and being part of a team to open it made me feel like I belonged. I was hanging with all these hot weightlifters who were younger than me, and they didn't care that I was divorced. I wasn't judged like I was by most of the people that lived up there. They just loved me and my two kids, and they became my posse. I built a community around myself and around the kids that made me feel strong and safe.

I finally went and got my real estate license and became a

licensed realtor and I could start slowly but surely trying to sell homes. It was very hard to break into the market up there because it was so inundated with all these people that had been in the business for forever. I was sort of shunned because I was divorced and I didn't have a lot of money. I remember feeling a lot of shame. It's funny the lies you tell yourself. Now that I look back they hadn't walked in my shoes and they didn't pay my bills so why did I care so much what they thought about me!

I loved my crew. The Asian flavor is what I called my two girls that were sisters. Those two girls would take my kids and I over to they're gorgeous mansion and their mother would cook for us and they just treated us like family. That's what we needed was to feel loved and not judged. They were always there for us and never treated us any different than anyone else. I found people that I could confide in and be myself and wouldn't judge me.

After almost a year of dating I was desperate for Dustin to tell me that he loved me and that he couldn't handle life without me. I bought some ecstasy thinking that if I gave it to him he would finally tell me how he felt. How desperate is it to want so badly for someone to tell you that they love you that you're willing to give them drugs.

So that night we took it and yes he said he loved me. As the night went on it seemed like the party just kept getting bigger. The music was playing loud, we were dancing and somebody handed me a glass of orange juice. I found out later that it was GHB and I drank all of it. I just didn't have my brain on that's for sure. The next thing I knew someone gave me something else and I didn't know what that was but apparently that was ketamine. That's why we have to constantly stay alert because evil comes when your blinders are off.

I saw my boyfriend in the distance in this dark club 250-pound bodybuilder falling all over the place like a bull in a China cabinet. Here I go with my little tiny mini skirt, super stilettos on and I put him on my back. I literally put him on my back and walked through the night club and walked him outside to our car. I knew in my brain that if I could just get him to my car that he would be fine.

The next thing I knew I woke up in the hospital with a tube down my throat and a catheter in my who-who and needles in every artery. I just remember opening my eyes and the flashlight came in my face. The Dr. said, "she's back, I think she's here for good this time." I remember thinking, is this a dream? They pulled the tube out of my throat and they told me I'd been dead on and off for hours. They didn't know if they would be able to pull me back! Someone slipped some- thing in your drink. I was shocked. Here is the sad part of where my brain was when I became coherent. All I could think about is where my pink Prada boots were? When the ambulance found me they cut them off. I wasn't thinking about how I almost died or where I was at that moment.

About an hour after they took all the needles and tubes out of me my good friend called and said they had put my boyfriend in jail for the night. They thought that he drugged me. This is how sideways your life goes when you aren't walking with God in any way. Self-caused drama!

My boyfriend and his buddy picked me up and I just put on whatever was there at the hospital and I left without even checking out. That was the day that would change everything and was my turning point. Years later I can remember me being on the ground and looking down at my body as I laid there helpless. I could see myself from above getting loaded into the ambulance and all my friends crying. I can tell you I didn't see any bright tunnel and that was a wakeup call for real.

Chapter 12

ON THE ROAD AGAIN

This was one of the weekends Theodore had the kids. I felt lost without the kids, the 6 days a month that I didn't have them. After I woke up at the hospital on the gurney in the ER I opened my eyes and heard the Dr. saying, "she's back, she's back!" with a flashlight in my face. As soon as all the tubes were out and I was wheeled into a room that wasn't the ER, I was out of there.

I literally just left the hospital without checking out at all. I knew the only place I could turn where I felt peace was the church. I usually sat in the back and I let the kids go to Sunday school and sometimes I would leave and go to Starbucks because I just had so much guilt.

That day the kids weren't with me, thank God, and my boyfriend went home and I went straight to church. I showed up with Band-Aids on my arms from all the IVS, bruises on my chest from the defibrillator, and a hoarse voice from the tube being stuck down my throat. I didn't care who knew or what anyone thought. I just wanted to praise God for saving my life even though I didn't feel at that time I deserved it. God has always loved me like a Dad is supposed to love their daughter with unconditional love. That morning I just knew the only answer that I had was to go to God. I didn't really realize I was a daughter of the

Creator of the world. I always felt like an orphan because of the rejection I felt from my Dad.

I always knew my Mom loved me and my family did but I never felt loved or adored or any of those things you are supposed to feel from my Dad. I always felt like something was wrong with me because I felt rejected and abandoned by my own Father. I still knew at that moment the only answer was to go to church. I hadn't really had the revelation yet that Jesus was and still is Abba.

When I pulled up in the parking lot of the church in my gold lifted Durango I hadn't slept all night. I'm sure I probably still smelled like urine and puke. I just needed to be where I knew I would feel peace. Of course right when I pulled up I saw the pastor. My pupils must have looked just like I had been in a dark room for days and my pupils were like pinholes. I'll never forget he looked right into my eyes and told me, "Polly I watch you every week. God has such a call on your life. I'll tell you what breaks my heart and your Heavenly Fathers heart is that you allow yourself to get a little bit close to Him, then you just have that spirit of rejection that you don't think you're enough for God's love and you run from Him.

He asked this question that I knew came directly from God to my ears, "when are you going to stop getting so close to God and then the moment your breakthrough is there you run away? You've been blessed so far but one day your life could be taken from you in a snap and you didn't even reach your calling."

My eyes filled up with tears and I knew at that moment I had to change my life. I couldn't continue going to church, and having sex with my boyfriend on the weekends, and doing drugs, and being a wild lukewarm person. I had to pick life or death. Somehow I thought I had earned being able to still have 2 feet in 2 different worlds. Since, by the way, I had survived a toxic marriage, and now I was a super mom 26 days a month. I thought I earned those four days that I got off a month, and those days I could party like a rock star. I was entitled to fun! I felt like I deserved something like this. That's what happens when we finally think we are free from something that doesn't make us happy. I thought if I partied hard and whopped it up like in my 20's that those things would actually make me feel fulfilled.

I have a question for you. Do you struggle to believe that you are pleasing to God just the way you are with all your flaws? Do you believe you were indescribably irresistible to Him? What obstacles if any do you recognize in your heart or thinking that keep you from receiving God's approval in your life?

I came from the old way of thinking that if I was just pretty enough, or fun enough, or cool enough or had the right stuff, that I would be fulfilled and that left me on the ground dead with nobody around me. I ask you to invite His perfect peace and bring that perspective into your circumstances. Just meditate on the fact that He is working everything together for good. It was so hard for me to grasp that back then, I felt like I deserved all the bad things. I didn't get the depth of God's love for me, no matter how badly I screwed up or messed my life up. If you don't know the Him I'm talking about, just close your eyes and ask yourself the deeper questions about what you do to be fulfilled with true joy and whether it is truly fulfilling. I can assure you partying and thinking it was fun put me on a sidewalk with my skirt above my waist, dead with strangers looking at me on a gurney....

I broke up with my boyfriend a few weeks later. Actually, God blessed me, and he ended it with me. At the moment I was devastated and I didn't understand. He told me he couldn't handle getting married again and that's what I wanted.

That took some guts. He could have strung me along for a long time. Blessings come all the time but when we are in the middle of what we THINK we want and it doesn't work out how we planned it feels so disappointing.

I remember being happy God saved my life but I thought he must be a fairytale. I put my hope in a person. At this point I'm alive (barely), the boyfriend is gone and I'm working. I'm going to church all the time, trying to piece my life back together God's way.

Meanwhile my ex-husband had met this woman and they were starting a relationship. The market was hot so I got my real estate li- cense and I started selling a few homes. My ex-husband signed a loan for me to get a home. We always had a pretty good relationship, more like brother and sister after we broke up. Besides when he would give me child support and sometimes spit at me.

The kids were going to get their own beautiful room in this gorgeous home, and we were so excited. Move-in day was like Christmas. The kids had their own bedroom, we got to decorate the house how we wanted. I thought back to that moment at church and the revelation of how I needed to change. I also thought back to being so sad when my boyfriend broke up with me, and I couldn't believe how things were turning around. It's the **sudden lies** that give you hope.

Things were really changing, Carmen had her basketball goal in the backyard, we had two turtles, and we could walk to school every day down the hill. During that time the market was starting to change in real estate. This was when you could get a loan even if you worked at 7-Eleven for a $500,000 home with barely anything down. I had sold a couple homes and got commission, so that with child support and alimony I could afford the bills. I was barely getting by, but I justified that with the fact that now I had a home just with the 3 musketeers.

About 8 months after moving into our dream home, the bubble burst in the real estate market, and for my ex-husband also. He lost his job, and I lost all of my clients and most of my child support. Ted was starting to slowly not get the kids as often on the weekends as his relationship got more serious. While I was living there, I dated a couple of guys, one in particular, his name was Chris. He was wonderful. He wanted to be a Dad to my two kids, and he was so sweet to both of them. He checked all the boxes. I just didn't quite have that feeling for him. I feel like I just wasn't ready to accept someone that loved me and my kids like we were his own kids. I still had it that I wasn't enough. Things were tight in the new house, and Chris would fill up our refrigerator and pay our utilities even after we broke up. God was always taking care of us now that I look back. One time my best friend Dondrea paid my electricity bill and filled my fridge without me knowing. I will never forget that! I love you girl...

Then the crash happened, and we had to sell that house and move into a little apartment right around the corner. I remember having to give away our turtle and a lot of our furniture. The kids were saddest about giving the trampoline away. Our neighbor right behind us had 3 kids. They said they would keep it till we got on our feet. I was devastated inside because the dream I had of a home with kids running around and jumping on the trampoline was disappearing right before my eyes.

Both my kids were super involved in children's ministry. We went on Saturday night, Sunday and Wed. I was leading a divorce single's group that I called the land of the misfit toys. I found peace in that group because they understood a single Moms' struggle.

Our awesome basketball goal that Carmen loved was going to have to go too. We could have sold it, which we needed the money for, but the kids wanted to donate it to the church for all the kids. Even in their lack they wanted to give.

Times were tough and Ted was paying slowly but surely and we barely had groceries at the new apartment. My Mom lived 25 minutes away so she couldn't just jump over. The kids shared a large bedroom upstairs and they had their own bathroom. The neighborhood had a great playground and pool so the sting of losing our things wasn't so bad. I feel God put us somewhere to ease us into each shift in our life that was coming. I was still a Girl Scout leader, and both kids were still in karate 3 times a week.

We had a great community. The karate studio called Family Karate knew we were struggling to pay every month. That was the one thing in the kid's life that stayed consistent though all the changes. They had been there for 3 years religiously. One day the owners asked if we needed a scholarship so we could continue. In a little over a year and half since the divorce I was needing a scholarship. I was humbled, embarrassed and grateful all at once. We accepted the scholarship and the kids never knew until later in life. I didn't want them to know how broke we truly were. I just tried to keep on plugging along.

I was still working part time at LA fitness and doing real estate. Money was tight and the church would bring us groceries a lot but I just kept the kids in that area because I knew that that's what they needed was stability. I'll never forget one of the Girl Scout trips I took Carmen on. I was always the co-leader. I was considered a fun mom. I couldn't be an organized mom because I just had too much on my plate.

This particular trip my Mom was watching Wesley and we went out to the little campground with all the other girls. Watching those women pack all of the cars with all the gear with all the supplies for ten girls for a weekend adventure with all the different activities planned was spectacular and I was in awe. If you are a Girl Scout or you're thinking about being in the Girl Scouts, I highly suggest it. Truly was a God sent for our family when we were really having a hard time. It's an amazing organization that helps teach women how to really get the job done.

Like I said I was always a fun mom trying to prove something I guess. This particular evening, we stumbled upon a very tall rope swing. I would watch people climb 10 feet up this log and grab the rope and jump and swing across the area below the tree. This area was also a walkway for campers to go to the bathroom. I watched one girl after the next swing on this super fun rope swing. Since I was the "fun" Mom everybody kept asking me to do it so of course I couldn't resist proving my title.

I climbed up on this tree and I motioned to all the Girl Scouts, "hey everybody! I'm going to do it." Now this rope swings, if you swing down, you're going really fast and you go literally right across the walkway where people walk right past so you have to be careful. Remember it was dark out and when I jumped of course my daughter was the one that walked across the path.

Just my luck, an epic fail on cool Mom territory. She didn't see me and I knocked her out cold and she got a concussion. Oh my gosh just the things that I've been through with these kids over the years was crazy but never boring. My poor little girl was such a trooper after the paramedic inspected her and she got some Motrin and ice. We were out roasting marshmallows on the fire. She was always such an easy going girl!!

My son tried sports but that really wasn't his thing. I'll tell you later why he just never was into it. I was his soccer coach for the years while he played rec soccer exactly for 5 long years. Wesley was also in Boy Scouts so he could have some mentoring I couldn't really give him. I was the camping Mom that went on most of his Boy Scout camping trips. I remember one trip, he and I were in our tent and I could hear all the dads with their sons in their tents. I cried myself to sleep that night wishing my son had that. It was a frigid night and we slept in one sleeping bag to stay warm. I felt much better in the morning when all the other boys said they froze all night. At least if I couldn't be Dad too I could nurture him and he was the warm one all night lol.

What he loved more than anything was Civil War reenacting. I know that what he was really looking for was some kind of Dad figure in his life to go to those things. I was okay with being the runner up. I would take him all over the state to go to these reenactments. I was able to slowly but surely with my Mom's help get him all of his Union gear so he could have all the right equipment when we would get there. When we would get to these wonderful reenactments they would literally look like the 1800s. There were canvas tents everywhere, no electricity, people were using lanterns and then on the third day they would have a battle.

Every reenactment was different, and the two sides, the North and the South, would somehow reenact a battle from the Civil War exactly how it played out in history. A sweet man named Arnold, who is no longer with us, took Wesley under his wing. He was the sergeant for our brigade. He was about 60 years old and was sympathetic to my son because he was raised by a single Mom too.

Through all my divorced years, God always brought someone into my kid's life to ease the burden and guilt I felt because their dad wasn't around. I didn't understand the concept and how to relay it to Wesley that he had a Father in Heaven that was pulling all the strings to make sure these cool men would show up in his and his sisters life. At all these reenactments I would just sit in my chair and let him go and do all of his soldier duties. It was a ball but I know deep down he was just looking for his dad to be there not me. Looking back, I wouldn't trade those sweet days for anything and I wish I appreciated it more when I was in it. After being in that little apartment and still trying to keep it all together we just couldn't do it anymore. One of my best friends from Girl Scouts needed help too, and they said we could move in with them. Here we go again round 3, I loaded up another U-Haul and put most of our stuff in storage right in that neighborhood. My plan was to only have it in there for 6 months while I got it together financially. It's funny how we make plans and we don't even have the chess pieces. Moving day was fun. Each kid had their best friend right there in the same house. God gave me a nice down cushioned pillow so every time we took a new step that felt like a step down at the time it would lessen each blow that was coming. I put both kids in one bedroom, and I had another bedroom all to myself. They had a beautiful home with a big family living area that we shared with their family and for eight weeks it was wonderful. The kids had someone to play with and everything was great. We felt safe. We were helping each other like a village raising kids together. Besides the 15 lbs. I gained from her husband's wonderful Persian cooking. We were doing good.

I'll never forget on Carmen's 11th birthday we felt the deep sense of a community wrapping their arms around our family. I couldn't afford much as far as a present went and I didn't know if Theodore was going to come or not and I didn't know if he was going to get her a present either.

It's funny every time I worry and have anxiety things always work out better after I'm through the storm. I have learned the more you let go and let God avoid so much stress. We really aren't in control of other people. That's how God operates. He doesn't show us the end to the beginning, that's where faith comes into play... At her birthday party in their backyard all the girls got together and saved their money and they bought Carmen a brand new bicycle. We were totally shocked and in so much awe of the sweetness of everyone.

She just cried, which was rare for her. I could see in her face that she understood that she was getting what she wanted even though I couldn't give it to her. I could see in her sweet little face it just touched her heart at the perfect time and in the perfect way. Jerimiah 29:11, "For I know the plans I have for you to prosper you not to harm you. To give you hope for tears." That's what we experienced that day. We had lost two homes, a car, another apartment, turtles, and her room. All her stuff was in storage, and at that moment, all that pain we had all put to the side was canceled.

New hope was present in all of us. I'll never forget that moment. Thank you to Girl Scouts of America because without that organization we wouldn't have had all those awesome girls in my daughter's life.

Their dad showed up just for a little while with his new girlfriend and he told us that he didn't have a job anymore. Like I said God al- ways gives us some kind of cushion to soften the blows life throws at us. You just have to look for blessings in the rain. I was just barely getting by at LA Fitness and selling real estate when the market tanked. We went from joy and hope back to despair. After that precious birthday party, Carmen and I both were crying because now we didn't know what we were going to do.

All I know is God always had our back through all of it, the good, the bad, the crazy. He was always right beside us. I'll never forget my sweet little girl looking up at me and saying, "mama, we can start over again and if we have to leave I know we're going to be OK mom. See Momma, God gave us that bike to show us how much He loves us and He will never leave us."

Out of the mouth of babes is truth. In that moment of despair again the scripture came to my mind for out of the abundance of the heart the mouth speaks, both of my kids always had good things that came out of their mouth when they were little they believed everything was always going to be OK. I know now looking back and they are both grown now that those 2 going to church and being involved with helping others even when we were in need is why they had such faith.

They were the wind beneath my wings. When I was in the middle of the storm I was so caught up in the business of trying to keep it together in a neat little package. Now I see how much the Holy Spirit dwelling inside of them helped me continue to get up every day.

Sometimes with my group at church and our outreach I would take the kids to what was our skid row. Lots of homeless drug addicts. My kids would give them food and clothes and pray for them and they were still little. It's that training at a young age that shaped them to even give me hope!

I want you to invite the Holy Spirit to expose any areas in your life where you desire to grow in humility and live in trust and delight of being like a child with your faith. *If you're worried about anything in your life, confess it to God and allow Him to bring His perfect peace perspective in your circumstances.*

Meditate on the fact that He is working everything together for good. I wish when I was in the middle of that storm I could've felt that and someone could've said that to me. I was frantic most of the time living in scarcity mode, and fear of messing my kids up because I got divorced, I pushed myself to get them to every single extracurricular thing I could to be a super Mom.

I was in performance mode constantly out of love for my kids but also out of fear of not being enough. That's when my autoimmune disease started. We manifest sickness sometimes by not dealing with our inner storm.

My storm was inner turmoil (the devil) constantly saying in my soul I'm not enough so I have to perform and do so I'll be enough and no one will know how I really feel because then I'll be alone.

That abandonment thing that came from my relationship with my Dad manifested itself in my life all the time. I am just now getting my identity is not about my Dad's non love but my identity is from heaven.

I'll never forget just feeling like I had ulcers in my stomach and what I was going to do. Trust me, after the birthday party was over and everything was cleaned up that night I sat up at the end of my bed after the kids went to sleep shaking and crying in fear. I went to God and prayed but I didn't know how to receive His peace. Please don't let that happen to you. There's nothing you're going through that God can't handle. I'm not saying you will wake up and everything will be perfect.

I'm saying the peace that surpasses all understanding will comfort you through all of it. You just have to ask and receive it.

At this point I had not gone back to school yet I was trying to figure everything out. I had applied for so many jobs and I was just waiting on answers. I had hoped for one really great job. My mom called me and she said Polly why don't you move down here with me? I have an extra room upstairs and until you get it together you can come be with me.

My mom's always been my rock no matter what I can always depend on her. So that afternoon two days after my daughter's 11th birthday I started packing all of our things and putting them in storage.

It was summertime, thank God. That meant the kids could start at a brand new school without having to start in the middle of the year. They had been in this area for everything since they were babies.

That feeling of being grateful we had somewhere to go, and feeling like the biggest loser definitely over lapped. Now you have to remember I still had Carmen's easy bake oven because she still liked to do those kinds of things, all of my son's fire trucks and matchbox toys. I wasn't about to throw those out because that would mean I was believing the next time we undid our storage they would be too old for all that stuff. I packed up everything except our clothes and some toys and this time put it all into storage. I thought it would only be there for six months this time for sure and we could move back up there. Little did I know how long it would truly be there. It's the end of summer and our village time is ending. The car was packed again with all our stuff to go to Gram-mommy's and we were off. I hung on hard for those 3.5 years after the divorce to keep the kids in the only environment they knew. That chapter was closing.

Again the soft pillow was going to Grandma's house. The kids felt comfort and peace there. We moved that day only 30 minutes south of our cute suburban neighborhood. To a cute little beach town called Point Loma. It could have been another state because we were truly starting over. Both kids were going to be changing schools and I was praying I was going to get a real job because there was no child support at all coming in anymore. Even though I've had that amazing experience where the pastor touched my hands after I died that day 2 years before the moving day and told me that God had a plan for me, that memory was vague and stored in the back of my mind. Through all the shuffling around and everything being so crazy I just didn't understand anything anymore. This time I had to truly Let go and let God. I knew I was being led once more and I just had to go with it.

Chapter 13

THE UPPER ROOM

I will never forget the day we pulled up at my mom's house in my lifted Durango with all our stuff packed in the back. We were all thinking we were only going to be there for a little while until I could afford to move us into our own place. It was right before school was starting and it was still summer. As we moved all of our belongings to the third floor of my Mom's town- home the feeling of defeat settled in. The lie that I kept telling myself was that I must be a loser that I couldn't provide a home for my kids on my own, and filled my heart and mind with such shame. When feelings like that come up you know that's not from your Creator. I wish I would have stopped that self-hate talk that day.

If we could only see the end from the beginning maybe, we wouldn't fret so much in the moment. The feeling of gratitude and being thankful occupied the other part of my heart at the same time. We had one bed in that upper room and one closet. The rubber had met the road and it was time for us all to press in and do it, suck it up and get it done. In the very beginning it was magical we had our entire family together. Welsey went to school right around the corner. Carmen had just started the sixth grade at a brand new school. I would walk her into school every day because the kids were click and she was the new kid and they had been going to school together for years. I loved that time with her watching her teachers talk about what a great girl she was. Watching her make lemonade out of lemons was amazing.

Wesley had been in and out of speech therapy for years. This new school presented a new opportunity for him. I knew I could hold him back in the second grade if we moved schools and no one would know so he repeated the second grade that year. This meant he could test again for the gifted program which I knew he would thrive in because it was a more individualized curriculum.

I found out within the first week of living there that I finally got a job. I was going to be working for a security company called Dunbar and I was going to be their sales representative. This meant I had flexibility because I was in outside sales with a nice salary plus commission and full benefits. I had hope now of being able to get our own place again and soon. Things were starting to look up and I was constantly planning our next move.

Then one night about a month after we moved in I heard my car alarm go off. I was 45 days late on my car payment. I knew once I got a paycheck I could catch up with the payments. I called my ex in laws. They were the kids' grandparents and asked if they could help me with one payment so I didn't lose my car since their son wasn't paying me anymore and they said no. I was too embarrassed to tell my Mom how destitute I really was so I never asked her to help me like that. I felt she was already doing enough. That night the car repo guys came. I went outside to ask if I could get my things out. I had those killer rims on the car that weren't factory. I knew when in need Sew a seed, so I did. As I walked outside with my head down I looked at the guys breaking into my car to take it. I said "hey you guys should take those wheels and put some factory ones on and at least make a little extra money for having such a crappy job." They looked at me like a deer in the headlights. I got to pray for them that night and tell them it wasn't their fault. They both cried at 4 am outside my Moms. They asked me if there was any way I could make a payment because they had compassion for me. I told them no, it was too expensive for me and this is better. I never knew if they actually took those tires or not.

I never had a Dad I could rely on at all. I always had my Heavenly Father and that night even in the middle of my prized lifted Durango getting repossessed I knew I was going to be ok. I was constantly taken care of because God could see my heart. He is a good Dad but you have to look at it like that constantly. See, I didn't pay my payments and it wasn't God's fault my car was taken away. God still provided for us because the next day a good friend called and said they had a car and I could pay them later. It was a 96 blue 300 SE Mercedes. I called it my dream car.

Looking back, I could have planned for the future but I was learning to live in the moment and trust God more and more on my journey. I couldn't have orchestrated all that if I tried. I couldn't afford that car on my salary and God knew that.

At this time the ex-had started to slip further and further away. I knew that drugs were involved. I just didn't know how deep. My child support payments were pretty much gone. Everything except having to pay rent was on me. That Durango would have meant I couldn't have provided a lot of the things the kids needed at my Moms.

We had been back-and-forth to family court so many times I already had an entire book full of filed paperwork with the state. At this point the kids were supposed to go every other weekend and that was starting to become less and less as he was becoming more and more unreliable. That first year at my Moms was really about balance, every Friday night we would all sit at home and decide what restaurant we were going to go to. Sweet Carmen always had to give in and she hardly got to pick where we would go to eat because her little brother was a lot angrier than she was at everything. It's almost like he had even more resentment.

I can remember one particular night when he didn't agree on what restaurant we were going to go to and he laid on our car as I drove down the street with him on it for a little ways. It was in the driveway and I was barely rolling but you get my drift. He got his way and she had to give in.

I had so much resentment penned up because all the responsibility was always pinned on me. I wasn't really doing the escape thing any- more. I knew I was it. The kids needed me 100% and whatever I need- ed for me needed to go on the way back burner. I know now I wish I would have sucked it up and been able to parent better and not give into the squeaky wheel little brother almost every time.

Carmen if you ever read this I'm so sorry I wasn't more conscious of how that must have made you feel. I want to thank you for always trying your hardest at everything to make my life easier. You were truly an angel. You live and learn and navigate the best you can, especially being a single parent.

Wesley I'm sorry I didn't know what you needed so you weren't always needing more. I wish I had a better skill set of handling your strong willed personality back then. My big plan was to give into what- ever you wanted and then lose my temper. I wish I could have been more rational back then and I'm sorry if I ever said things that stuck. Please know that doesn't excuse my behavior. I just want you to know I was reacting and it wasn't ok and I'm sorry.

I became Salesperson of the Year at Dunbar that year, Carmen was in choir at Dana Middle school and we went on several different choir adventures. She won many awards. I know that was a life saver for her at that school. Wesley finished the second grade and was now in Gate seminar (gifted program) because he was able to test for that. Being able to be in the Gate seminar was another blessing of the move. I kept a book called God's provision. I did this so I could focus on the blessings and not beat myself up over not being able to provide better for the kids. Who would've thought a kid that was in speech his whole life and now he's in the gifted program that made it in my God's provision book. God can turn around your situation in an instant.

Second grade went by and sixth grade went by for the kids. I'll never forget her sixth grade graduation and how terrified I was of her being upset because her Dad might not show. I overcompensated by buying enough balloons and trying to put on the mask that everything was perfect just so she wouldn't notice if her dad

didn't show up. Halfway into the ceremony I looked over and there he was. I had so much anger and resentment I couldn't stand that he was even there but I knew that made her happy.

I am still working on needing recognition all the time. I've let go of a lot of the anger I had for him leaving after we split up and kind of checking out. What I've learned in the 10 years since this time in my life is to do everything knowing that you will get your recognition one day from God. I once again had to suck it up and go out to eat that day and pretend like everything was perfect even though I knew he had been up to no good. It's that crumb mentality that comes from not having a Dad. I even felt crumbs were enough for my kids just like my Mom thought it was for me. My Mom would take me to go see my Dad in prison when I was younger just so I could have some kind of relationship with him. Mind you, I went to probably 4 or 5 different federal prisons all over the country for crumbs. God says you are His kids and I'm pretty sure if you're the Creator of the universe kids you deserve more than crumbs.

As a single Mom I didn't know about boundaries or peace. One particular weekend when he was supposed to get them I'll never forget their little faces when they said, "mom just leave us outside." Those 2 sat on the corner with their suitcases and I kept looking out the window with my mom wondering if he was ever going to come. I let an hour go by, two hours went by and by the third hour I walked outside and I said, "guys it looks like he must be busy. Do you want to go get some ice cream?"

The fighting would become so intense between the kids sometimes I felt like I wasn't going to make it. I had so much misplaced anger that I didn't know where to put it all. Food and going out to dinner with Mom (the other parent) was my go to so as to alleviate all the pain we were all feeling but didn't know how to express it. I would try to cover up all the disappointment and unkempt promises and commitments that he caused and pretend like everything was fine. Pushing down feelings and sweeping them under the rug just gives room to them rearing their ugly head in other places in your life.

I would ask myself how he could do this and that he is totally abandoning us and sticking me with everything. A repeat of what my Mom went through I am sure. The only difference is we thought he was dead till I was almost 16. I don't know what's worse. A Dad who's alive but gone or a Dad who was supposedly dead and got raised from the dead.

It always really felt like he was abandoning us even though I asked for the divorce, but now it was even more evident that he was slipping even further away. I knew drugs were involved but I just didn't know the extent yet. I felt powerless most times. I had a lot of guilt for getting divorced and for picking a guy that would do sort of what my Dad did.

I just worked hard and focused on what I could control. I woke up 30 minutes before the kids every morning. I would go to the bathroom in our upper room and read the Bible. Then I had 15 minutes on my

knees by the bathtub in that little bathroom to pray. Those moments are what gave me hope for our future and the courage and strength to keep persevering. I honestly don't know what I would've done in those years without that time with God.

Carmen got into the school right around the corner from my mom's house so she could walk to school every day. My Mom was amazing and she wrote a special letter to the director. My Mom helped develop her neighborhood and she had a lot of pull.

This was a charter school that was more about group learning and it was more intimate. I knew my baby girl would thrive there.

Wesley had started volunteering at the Church which was right around the corner. He would walk over there and volunteer from 5am- 9pm at night. He started out being the stage manager there. This is a church that is filmed and shown to over 150,000 people every Sunday. Carmen was in charge of the prayer team at her school in seventh grade and it was a charter school that was all about empowering kids to learn how to work in groups.

The kids having another environment surrounding them that made them feel safe was a good thing. You know that sweet song, "He's got you and me baby in His hands." That's what I felt constantly.

I would still drive Carmen up to Karate and to Girl Scouts once a week in 4S Ranch and I had found a Boy Scout program there in Point Loma for Wesley.

Seventh grade passed and third grade passed and now my son is in fourth grade and my daughter is in eighth grade the year before high school. Theodore had not paid me at all for almost a year and a half. I had every other weekend and I would pray that he wouldn't show up. The cleanup job with the kids regardless if he came or not wasn't ever fun.

Things were a mess when I would have to let them go over to his house and I never knew what was going to happen when they were with him. I had to let go and let God. That was the hardest part for sure. I had them on a routine at home and they felt stable. I stopped letting them go over there after this one particular weekend.

Carmen begged me to please let them go over there that they would be fine she was 11 and Wes was eight and this woman he was dating's daughter was there and their newborn baby of seven months old. This was my kid's half-brother and they loved him so much. I re- member calling all that Friday night and Carmen would answer their phone and tell me everything was OK. I called all morning Saturday and she would say, "We're OK, I'm OK mama they're just still upstairs doing paperwork." For an entire 48 hours I knew something was really wrong.

I had an old love in my life that had come into my world that I had not seen since I was a young girl in Newport Beach. His name was Steve and I called him surfer Steve and that particular weekend he took me away to Vegas. It was a magical trip. I felt the beauty of feeling like a beautiful woman again and feeling free even though I was worried the entire weekend because my kids were with their dad. I guess ole Steve was a distraction. I was so unsure of what was going on all weekend but the whole situation was completely out of my control and there was nothing I could do to get them away from him that weekend. We had been to family court so many times and I had finally filed a restraining order that got dismissed and everything else to try to protect them but all I could do was put them in God's hands.

I had not really been dating at all since I lived at my mom's because I didn't get very much free time. I spent my days going to work and then picking up the kids and taking them to whatever different events they had and I kept myself really too busy for any kind of dating. It wasn't my mom's job to babysit my kids while I go out and have some life on the side and she was kind enough to let us live there and the last thing I needed to do was take advantage of her. This weekend the kids were gone and Steve said that I was the love of his life so he took me away to Vegas for the weekend. My stomach was in knots all weekend thinking that the kids were in some kind of danger but I couldn't do anything.

That's the way the courts are. If you can prove that without a rea- sonable doubt the kids are in physical danger then you can do some- thing about it but I couldn't prove anything at this point. I just had calendars full of missed dates. I had times recorded when he was sup- posed to show up and he didn't. This went on for two solid calendar years. There was disappointment after disappointment that the kids had. All they really wanted was their dad. They weren't about to tell me anything bad about their Dad because they knew I would not let them go over there anymore and I would fight for them in court. I had nothing except no child support, and missed dates. This particular weekend, Steve and I went away and we saw a Vegas show, we played in the sun at the pool, we went to this amazing church there was even a warm rain, and we played in it, and it felt like it was days. It was literally only 24 hours. It felt like an eternity because I hadn't had real me time in so long.

I left to come home exhausted and happy that I wasn't full of anxiety, even for a little bit, about the kids. On the way home, I started hearing the song "He Reigns," and I could feel the Holy Spirit fill my car. This feeling was unlike anything I had ever felt, and the presence of the Lord was so strong I had to pull over. It felt like I was safe, my kids were going to be ok, and I was at peace and protected, something I had not felt in years.

I checked into a hotel on the way home from Vegas because it was a 5 Hour drive to San Diego but I knew I didn't have to get my kids until the next day so I checked into a hotel room. I just remember that I started crying because I finally felt what it felt like to feel like a woman again. I had held in tears for years about everything and I finally had a place where I was alone and I could let it all out.

Steve and I did not have sex because I was committed to not having sex until I got married to anyone. I was on the Altar Call at church, I was doing mission trips with Carmen, and I was dedicated to really knowing the Lord at an intimate level.

That weekend I was a lot friskier than I felt like I should've been and I had all this guilt. Conviction is a good thing because repentance just brings you closer to oneness with God but guilt that sure ain't from your Heavenly Dad.

In the middle of my hotel room that night, I lay straight on the floor, and I cried to God and asked Him to forgive me. I asked for forgiveness for the weekend but also for all my resentment I had about everything and the anxiety I carried instead of trusting Him. I came to him like a beggar instead of a princess. I can remember so clearly laying there, and I could hear the audible voice of God that night in that hotel room all alone, and the smell of roses filled the room as I lay there. I heard the voice say, "Look up", and I looked up as I was lying on the floor, and I saw Jesus hanging on the cross, and He said, "You need to stop. Don't you know I finished it there? I would've done this if just for you. You are forgiven, and you need to let go. It is finished."

I have never felt an overwhelming sense of love, peace, forgiveness, clarity, and what it feels like to have love from a father. I didn't feel shame or condemnation or guilt, but it was just an admiration of wanting to hold my Heavenly Father in a holy place and not dishonor Him with my thoughts or my actions. I could feel the love of a Father I had never felt before. I felt loved, cherished, protected, forgiven, and accepted no matter what. That there was nothing I could ever do that would separate me from the love that He had for me. NOTHING! I had a kiss from Dad.

I left the next morning and went back to San Diego. I felt strong because I had that experience of my heavenly Father in that room and I knew no matter what I would walk into when I picked up my babies from their Dad that I would be OK.

That's the way God 's always operated in my life, like a Dad, like the kind of Dad I always wish I had but I never did. I picked up the kids that Sunday from their dad's and I knew something was different. My daughter told me that they were locked in that room downstairs all weekend and they barely saw their dad because he was too busy doing paperwork. That was the day that I filed the paperwork and it was accepted that the kids didn't have to go with him anymore unless I was there and I was a supervisor. Our court system needs to change!

I found out years later when I read my daughters essay to get into college what really happened. What happened that weekend when I had knots in my stomach was her dad was addicted to drugs and so was his girlfriend. The entire weekend they were upstairs doing drugs and were forgetting to feed the kids.

Carmen went upstairs alone after she didn't know what else to do to feed the baby. She found the keys with everyone passed out upstairs with drugs everywhere, got money out of her dad's pocket and went downstairs. She loaded up an eight-year-old, a seven-year-old and a newborn baby in a car and drove to the grocery store at 11pm. She got diapers, formula, and popsicles and some food and she drove about a quarter-mile in a car at 11 years old and came back and did it herself. Just thinking back to reading that letter for the first time when she was 18 and going to college still makes me cry. I wanted my kids to have a crumb from their Dad so bad that I didn't know what to do. I just thought that something even if it was sucky was better than nothing. I know angels were protecting them and me that weekend.

When my mom used to take me to prison to visit my dad, she thought the most important thing to me was for me to have anything from my dad that would somehow suffice for being abandoned and lied to.

I'm here to tell you that no kid deserves a crumb. That if you're a father and you're reading this, and you have been a crumb Dad I pray that it convicts you. **Your children need**

to be your priority and the love of your life. It forms how they feel about who they are; you are a big part of their identity.

Moms, if you have a dad that's being like this to your kids, you need to let your kids know they have a Heavenly Father that loves them, and their dad's behavior has nothing to do with them not being enough. **Kids, if you're reading this and you have a crumb Dad, it's not your fault. Hurt people hurt people without even realizing what they're doing.**

All I know is that if I would've known how much my Father in heaven loves me and how I am his daughter and my kids are his children, then maybe I could've imparted that more to my children so that all that disappointments from their Dad would have stung a little less. Nothing replaces a Dad trust me, I get it. **People need to know their Dad's absence, or unloving presence, or incapability to be there has nothing to do with them not being enough!**

So now Carmen is in ninth grade, Wesley is in fifth grade, and their Dad is hardly around anymore. Sports became a big part of Carmen's life, and I knew I could excel at helping her with that. She was super busy with volleyball, and I was able to help her on her team, and she was doing great. We would spend hours behind my Mom's house practicing serves and bumps for games. Our weekends were filled with volleyball games and her little brother following us around everywhere so that my mom could get a little bit of a break in the evenings.

By this time, Wes is no longer sleeping in the bed with me, and I have a little twin bed next to the queen bed. Carmen and I are still sharing a bed. I was so happy she could walk to her new high school, and it was literally 50 yards from our house. She was not quite as ashamed as living in one room as Wesley was.

His school was full of rich kids and he went to the local public school so it was a little bit more embarrassing to him. I had signed him up for the big brothers of America so he would have some male influence besides reenactments and Boy Scouts a few times a month.

His big brother was a nice guy who took him to fun places to eat and just hung out with him. Wesley was getting more and more involved in the broadcasting part at the church. That big brother thing was for a year. Just enough for him to grow up a little more.

I remember thinking now that I had my real estate license and I was still working at Dunbar so things are starting to do better so that maybe I could move out soon. I knocked on a bunch of people's doors in our neighborhood and I got three listings which was a miracle. I was working under a woman from church but little did I know that the woman that I signed up with had actually listed all the houses under her name and didn't tell me anything. Right before it was time to close on all 3 listings she got 100% of all the commission. Through her screwing me over I met one of the women that bought one of the homes. She really loved me and took me under her wing. I helped her buy 2 houses that year. I made what I lost on those listings. I saved that money so we could get our own place. That was just one of the many times I thought we were about to get our own place.

I signed up for some online dating site. There was a guy that I would talk to in Nebraska when I would run in the afternoons. He was a big talker and he would tell me how rich he was and how he was going to buy me and the kids a house. I would tell Wes that I found a good guy that was going to help us get a place and the money I made from the homes I sold we could save for a rainy day.

Of course he was full of it. I now think he probably lived in a trailer park in the middle of nowhere and got his kicks by luring women into believing his crap. I guess I was still a little desperate to get our own place and I again wasn't leaning into the Holy spirit I was pushing my plans not His. I can't even begin to tell you the roller coaster that my kids had in those seven years of how many times we thought we were going to move out because I just thought I couldn't take it anymore.

I would get up 30 minutes early every morning and pray on my knees in the bathroom that was connected to our bedroom. I called the toilet my holy throne because that's when I would read my chapters in the Bible. I read through the entire Bible every single year the seven years that we lived here. My time with the Lord was so intense and it is the only thing that got me through it. I would record the miracles in the small provisions in the small baby steps of how God would provide for us as a family and I would count the small blessings because some- times I just couldn't see it.

I kept that money for my commission as a move out fund. Again listening to my agenda and not God's agenda. We want what we want, when we want it but it's not always what's going to be best for us in the long run. God was constantly protecting me from myself.

Now that Carmen is in high school and it's almost the end of her ninth grade year and Wes is in fifth grade and he's almost done I had learned that I really wanted to be a teacher. I was going to work during the day and pick up the kids and take them to all their things until about 9 o'clock at night. After all that and dinner was picked up and they were situated. I would pop an Adderall and I would start writing my papers for school.

I decided I wanted to become a full-time teacher and I would change the world one kid at a time with health and nutrition. I had signed up over the past 2 years for a training seminar called Landmark. I learned that I was a liar and that being late all the time was rude. I also saw how I showed up in life and figured out how I could make a difference in the world. I was truly changing that inner dialogue from all my wounds as a child. Now it was time for me to quit my fabulous job in faith and become a teacher. I knew I could teach sports and nutrition and that would be truly fulfilling. So I quit my $80,000 a year job with all my benefits and stepped out in faith to teach school for free for six months.

In California to get your teaching credential you have to teach under a master teacher and not get paid. My kids knew that this would be a sacrifice, but again I thought this would be good for everyone. I thought we would be able to move out once I got a teaching job. I knew I would have all the same breaks with the kids and summers off. I had saved that money from those houses I sold. I knew that God had provided that for this time. That wasn't the case. God was protecting us for even more than I even knew and every time I thought that we were supposed to move out and we didn't God showed me exactly why we were still there. I call it stuck like purgatory but honestly it was a place of protection and provision.

Chapter 14

NEW STARTS: WHEELCHAIRS, ENGAGEMENT & DEATH

You never know what the universe has in store for you, you certainly can put your plans out there but somehow they always change.

You just have to keep focused on the prize and don't get distracted by the curveballs.

Finally, I finished everything I needed to do with teaching, all of my tests, I passed all of my classes and I finally got my assignment to become an intern. I prayed that I would get a school that was close to my kids so that I could pick them up in the afternoons and we would be on the same schedule. I was so sad to leave Dunbar. It has provided a great flexible schedule and stable money coming in. It was time to take a step off into the unknown and follow my passion and really step out in faith. I had spent 3 years in that room with the kids writing my papers to follow my real passion for health and nutrition and to change the dynamics of children's health in education going forward.

I got an internship at the middle school right around the corner from my son and only 10 minutes from Carmen's school. I taught seventh and eighth grade PE as an intern or student teacher, which means I had no money coming in. I was older than my master teachers I was under. I sat at a kid's desk in their stinky office and basically was their pledge for 6 months with no pay! I'm sure I was irritating to them because they had that office by themselves in the girl's locker room for a long time. I had to be right there so I could learn. I'll just say it was a humbling experience that's for sure. Sometimes you have to just suck it up and eat humble pie to go in a new direction. I just kept my eyes on the prize getting through it all.

I still had my real estate license but I applied for help from the government. Let me tell you something walking into a welfare office as a white woman I have never been shamed like I was that day. I saw everybody else there that had to hand in no paperwork but they asked me 1 million questions like I was some kind of criminal.

It was as if they thought there was no way I would need the help. To be quite honest our system is very racist. So now that I knew I could get food because I was able to get food stamps and I was living with my mom and I had some money coming in I could concentrate on the task at hand. The task being getting to my last hurdle before I could actually teach school and become a certified teacher.

I fell in love with the kids at that middle school. They were amazing and I could pick up my son from school. There is such power in being grateful. Gradually the teacher I taught under let me have a few classes by myself. It was great because I could bond with the kids. I was the 7th grade PE coach.

The bell would ring and the girls would pile in the locker room and change. Then we would walk out to the black top to take roll and stretch. I had a few kids I really got close to and am still close to one of them to this day. She is like a daughter to me and I would do it all over again if just to meet her. Summer, if you read this you helped me get through it all, you and Miss Aubrey.

During that time my Papa who was like a father to me since mine wasn't there passed away. One of my best friends back home told me that one of her friends was single. He was someone I knew from when I was young. When I went home to the funeral after so many years of being alone I thought, "Well, God, maybe this is what you're doing, maybe you're guiding me back home so that I can be back with all our family in Arkansas. I went on a date that day with Michael and felt that feeling again. He flew back-and-forth to California while I was student teaching.

My schedule was rigorous and my son was beginning to have health problems. Somehow we managed to get so close over a long distance. The third time I saw him I flew to Arkansas to really meet his whole family again. My family and his family lived in the same town and were friends. I felt like all the pieces were starting to make sense. Like maybe quitting my great paying job and becoming a teacher would be perfect. I could teach school anywhere. The second day I was there I woke up at his beautiful ranch style home. I slept in my own bed that night be- cause he knew I was a solid Christian lady and he truly was a gentleman and respected that. I woke up to roses in the kitchen and he told me he had something truly special planned for me that day.

That day was a beautiful sunny day with just a hint of the smell of fresh gardenias blooming in the air. We went to his friend's house on the Arkansas River. It was a monumental brick home with many acres of open space with a cow pasture right on the river, it was breathtaking. As we waited around I had no idea why we're waiting so long, like, were these people a close part of his life or what. Was this the special thing he had planned? As soon as I kind of was thinking like why are we sit- ting here with these people I heard the sound of a helicopter growing closer and closer. That's why we went there and why he was so nervous I finally got it. I had never been in a helicopter. As it landed in the open pasture he told me he couldn't fit but his friend was going to show me the city. We took off and we flew around the city, Little Rock. It was so small compared to San Diego.

We flew back over the cow pasture and the guy said look down. I didn't see anything so he made another loop. I looked down and Mi- chael had painted on many large boards," will you marry me"? I was in shock and so surprised the helicopter landed and there he was on one knee with a giant ring. I said yes, and was so happy.

It all made sense. All of the questions I had about all my decisions were clear at that point. He took me that afternoon and bought me an engagement outfit. I still had no idea why I needed a different outfit but I was so happy to go shopping, something I had not been able to do for a long time.

We pulled up to the restaurant that he told me about. I thought he and I were going to have a romantic dinner alone to celebrate. That was not the case at all. He had all of our mutual friends and family at the restaurant to say congratulations. It was the most precious thing I had ever experienced from a man. I felt like at that point all of my Land- mark and all of my fixing of my past daddy issues wounds were finally starting to be repaired. I left that day being engaged.

I went back to San Diego for my last part of student teaching and Wesley started having even more health problems. He was having a hard time at school with not being able to walk without extreme pain. Michael flew out one more time and I took him and my kids hiking and he just could not get along with my son. He stayed the night at my Moms and I noticed things that I didn't notice before that bothered me. Probably because I had really only physically been around him 2 times before we got engaged. Wes was having health problems to top off, so now I was rethinking this whole engagement move thing. I knew that moving away with the kids wasn't a good idea. I took him to the airport and we both cried because as close as we were we both knew our 2 worlds weren't ready for each other yet so I gave him his ring back.

My kids are and were first and they already lost one parent they didn't need to lose another. I believe in a weird way that was a blessing. I could not focus on moving and getting married and all the little de- tails because my son was about to go through two years of almost hell I didn't even know about at that point. Again, there's the curveball, just roll with it. God never gives you more than you can handle. Sometimes your mess turns into your message. Now looking back that is another characteristic of a good and loving dad making sure that you are guided even when you don't know it.

After coming home, I had 1 week till I was through with student teaching. I was very close to my son's school. The last day of teaching I got a call that my son couldn't walk. That day we rushed my son to the hospital. He had a genetic disorder called SCFE. Basically the top of his femur bone was slipping out of his hip and he could no longer walk. I finished student teaching just in time and I officially had my credential which was perfect timing. See, God knew from the end to the beginning even though in the middle of yet another let down (the break up with Michael) He knew my baby boy was going to need me 100%. Wesley had to have surgery and he was going to need full-time care.

Thank God I had that money that I had saved up from those houses I had sold in the beginning of student teaching and I had gotten Federal assistance because I was going to need it. We had the best insurance because we had Medi-Cal for kids called healthy families and all of his surgeries were covered. If I would have moved it would have taken time to get insurance, and Lord only knows how much that would have cost. I was being led without even realizing it at the time. It was like the Israelites when they were given manna from heaven as provision but they didn't even realize how provided for they were. My point is, count your blessings no matter what. Complaining is music to the devil's ears and complaining hinders God being able to answer your prayer because you are taking things into your own hands, instead of leaving it all in His hands. I still struggle with letting go of control but I am starting to see His hands are way bigger than I ever thought.

If we look at our lives, we can see how we are guided by a heavenly Father that loves us so much. We just have to allow Him to guide us and get out of the way. When we are raised not knowing the love of a Dad it's so hard to grasp the love of an invisible Dad and to trust He has our back. It was surgery time and his first surgery was a success and for six months we went back-and-forth to the doctors and physical therapy. I was getting by selling real estate part time. Their Dad was somewhat in the picture but no money, and no relief with all the schedules for both kids. Thank God, Carmen was doing great in school and sports. God only gives you as much as He knows you can handle. I was truly stretching my tent pegs and growing my faith on a moment to moment basis.

My entire life was Carmen going to Girl Scouts and selling cookies with her, taking her to all her games and practices, making sure my son got to all of his appointments, he still had Boy Scouts. Carmen was on the volleyball team doing great. I always clung to the promises of God and the preciousness of my sweet son and daughter when I would read their letters that they would write. We have to cling to the promises not the trials. This particular letter was written after my son just had his first surgery, how can I ever get upset with that. Wes was still able to take his wheelchair all the way over to the church and work and that was kind of his saving grace to get away from all of us women.

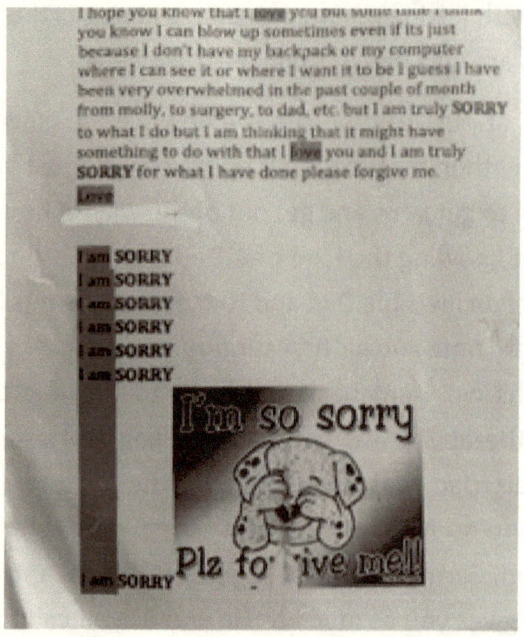

He had a little fight about something so insignificant and this is what I found on our bed. It was little moments like that I knew my kids were going to be ok and all the sacrifice was worth it.

We had LEGOLAND passes, Balboa Park passes, and the zoo pass- es. I was always called the fun Mom. One Halloween in particular I said let's go to LEGOLAND. Both kids thought that was wonderful because they could get into the fast pass lane because of Wesley's wheel- chair. What I figured out through my kid's resilience in that moment was I could complain and be pitiful or I could be powerful and be thankful that I have the time that I had to be with them. It's always a choice moment to moment what you focus on. Trust me in the middle of raising 2 kids by myself, going to school, living with my Moms, an ex that was not there and on drugs, my precious Mom helping me parent, I had every excuse to be pitiful. Or as my Meme would say, "sit on my pity pot." My saving grace was that 15 minutes in the morning before the kids woke up.

The final straw of trying to have my kid's dad in their life before Theodore finally went into his first real rehab was when I drove Wes to go to one of his civil war reenactments. He was living in an apartment in a super sketchy part of town. The building used to be a crappy hotel. It was a grey cinder block design 2 levels with about 40, 1 bedroom apartments surrounding a middle courtyard. Now that I think about it literally used to be super 8. The people that were staying there all had broken down cars and you could tell it was a drug hotspot for the area. He was living with his girlfriend.

My son begged me not to come to the reenactment. He was just done with his Mommy being there instead of his Dad. When I finally saw his dad I could tell he was high. He pulled up into a grocery store parking lot on a bicycle because he did not have a license anymore. My son had tears well up in his eyes because I know now he knew his dad was messed up and he knew if I knew I would not leave him and then he would be let down yet again. I felt uncomfortable leaving him but my son, with tears in his eyes, looked at me and said, "mom I have a phone I'll call you if anything happens. Driving away that day from my then 11-year-old was one of the hardest things I had done. I knew angels surrounded my kids so I had to trust that.

I found out years later that he never stayed in the tent with my son at that park. My 11-year-old stayed alone with all the reenactors and never told me so he could protect his dad. His dad spent the night doing drugs and the very next day they went to Walmart where my son was called on the loudspeaker at Walmart to come see his father zip tied Because of him trying to steal to get money to buy drugs. My little 11-year-old looked those officers in the eyes and said, "Please let him go, do you really think I need to go to foster care? My mom will be here any minute."

Those two took the bus home and my little baby boy, all 11 years of age, called me hysterical. I drove up there at about 120 mph an hour and a half trip took me 55 minutes. When I walked in the door it was all I could do to not smash his face in. My little boy was filthy and I could tell he had not eaten in 2 days. I drove him straight to Chipotle and he ate a large burrito and a full entire bowl. That ride home was so quiet I didn't want to ask him what happened because I could tell he was devastated.

That was when we flew his parents out here and did an intervention because I knew it was time or their dad was not going to make it anymore.

Finally, we all did an intervention and his parents flew out. Carmen and Wes sat in the hotel room and told their dad of all the different experiences they remembered when they were with him and how scared they were. My daughter said with tears in her eyes, "you remember the time you passed out behind the wheel and the car pulled over? We were hitting you to wake up. I was scared, dad, but I didn't let Wesley know what was wrong but I knew." I just broke at that moment. Every time my kids would go with their Dad I would pray for angels to surround their car. I knew that it was the angels that protected them that night. This brought him to his knees and he knew he needed help.

He went to a Christian rehab 1 hour away and we could visit him once a month. I would drive the kids up there so that they could visit with their father. He really had a good heart deep down and I knew that he could be a good Dad just like his dad. Sometimes we just have to break down to get a breakthrough. Ted had to be there at least 6 months to graduate and have the blessings from the pastors. I went on Christian mingle just to see if I could find one more good guy out there. I met this really sweet Christian man and I knew right away that it wasn't about dating but that he was going to help me in real estate so that I could be there for both kids. He took my son several times to go go-karting and paid for my car when it was broken down. I couldn't afford to get my brakes fixed on my car and he was there at the perfect time. My bill was well over $500.00 and that was way out of my budget. God always took care of us. He's such a good father. I had the flexibility I needed with real estate so that I could again be there for the kids and keep them focused not on their dad being gone once again. I know that another one of God's messengers, this man was a big blessing in keeping Wes occupied so he didn't think as much about his dad. Carmen was in 9th grade and was doing amazing. She worked so hard at her grades and was so supportive with all of her brother's surgeries. I believe her coping mechanism was to do her best at what she could control.

I'm so grateful to Rady's children's hospital. What a wonderful place. They took such great care of my son. Carmen and I got to stay at the Ronald McDonald house so that we could be right next-door. It was a big welcoming facility with a community kitchen where volunteers would prepare meals for families every day.

This is a children's hospital in San Diego that deals with many low income families. They treated us like we were just as important as any- one else. That place was a God sent.

At this time, their dad had just gotten out of rehab and graduated from his place and we had helped him move into a place right in town. my Moms. He needed his kids and they needed him. It was time for healing of hearts.

Things were going better in our lives and I believed this was going to be Wesley's final surgery. I was doing OK financially and I had the flexibility so I could be there for all of them. The guy that had been in my life ever since I got divorced was Chris. When I still lived in 4S Ranch he was my first nice guy to date after my break up with the bodybuilder. He came back into the picture and we had not dated in about eight years but he had always been in my children's life. He was a constant man that would come around and be there for us and do anything for us.

After the first relationship after I got divorced ended we dated for about 8 weeks. Then I really didn't date for about 4 years until Michael from Arkansas, then nothing until I got remarried.

I thought to myself after Chris was around a lot more, "well it didn't work out with Michael I didn't move to Arkansas maybe I am supposed to marry this man. He loves my children and he's a good person." He checked all the boxes. I decided before Wesley went into surgery that Christmas if he proposed that I would say yes. So that Christmas Eve I invited him over. I had no idea what his intentions were and he never showed. Wesley went into surgery on the 26th of December.

As the nurses were rolling Welsey out of surgery I got the phone call. I heard, "is this Polly?" I said yes, and they said, "I knew what Chris was planning on Christmas and I know now why he never showed." My voice got quiet wondering what had happened to him and why he never showed up on Christmas. That wasn't like him; he was always so dependable. The voice on the other end said "I'm sorry I have to tell you this, but Chris passed away suddenly on Christmas Eve and that's why you never saw him: We just found him today, that's why the call is now." I was in the ER with my son who literally was on a gurney and I

Then I rented a van and moved all of his stuff another 2 hours south and drove it to his new apartment. His place was about 5 minutes from got that phone call. I was speechless, how was I going to tell my kids, especially my daughter, she loved Chris.

He died suddenly in the shower as he was coming over to our house to propose. I have never felt so devastated. Here is my son coming out of surgery, their dad is sleeping on the floor in his room finally there for his kids and I'm trying to hold it together.

The Lord says He will never give you more than you can handle but that time in my life I felt like it was too much! I FELT SORT OF happy that their dad was finally there and what I thought finally was going to be the person I was going to marry and would be a wonderful father figure for my kids was gone. I cried myself to sleep that night in the Ronald McDonald house. My daughter was just as devastated if not more so than I was. She never understood why I didn't want to be with him, she loved him and I know that that broke her heart. She always just kept a sweet smile on her face to try not to cause any problems or any more grief. I couldn't be more proud of both of them for always rising above whatever it was. That seemed like the longest week ever. We got through another battle. Time was passing by and Wes was getting better, my heart was repairing. He was about to go into the seventh grade and Carmen was in the 10th. We had made a decision that summer that she would not do volleyball because she needed to do another tall girls sport and we put her in Rowing. How would I have known what a wonderful thing that was for her. Honestly it was divine direction that was just a suggestion from her doctor at her yearly physical. That decision led to so much joy for her and us and for her to have friends that she is still close to.

My son was healing and he was now in seventh grade. He had learned so much at the Church for three years on how to be an amazing director. He had moved his way up almost as a live video director at only 12 years old. He knew that his little school Correia needed a news team that made lemonade out of lemons. He used all that time when he was down in his room healing from all his surgeries to become so efficient on his computer.

He wrote a $10,000 grant and rebuilt their entire newsroom. I thought, "wow I'm never going to have to worry about him." They built the most amazing news room and middle schoolers got to have a news team that did the announcements every morning live. Pretty amazing!

Carmen had already made the A-Team and I knew with a 4.5 grade point average and all of the tutoring and support that she had through all of this that she was going to excel too.

That was it after Chris. I said no more men in my life. I just needed to focus. At long last I finally got my job at Farb Middle school and I was the PE teacher officially and I was going to get paid for it. Things were finally starting to come together.

Chapter 15

HE'S ALWAYS BEEN THERE!

At this point I felt positive all that hard work popping Adderall late at night so I could write papers, working during the day, driving the kids everywhere to everything was all starting to pay off. God's final objective for us is not resolving anything or getting well, His ultimate goal is maturing us into who He says we are and then releasing us into the dreams HE designed for us before the world began.

God carefully designed HIS influence system so that we would have influence far more out of who we are rather than what we do.

Slowly but surely I was healing and realizing that God's purpose for me was not just to be a mother but it was to be happy and fulfilled and walk into the destiny He designed for me. See, He wants to use our mess to make a message to bring healing to a hurt and dying world. That's why when people say, "if God is only good then why did you suffer so much?" That is the point to atonement. I recently wrote a paper on this and I could not understand what that meant. When Jesus died on the cross He took back the keys from Hell so that we would be in the right relation with the Father forever. How could a Dad love us so much still baffles me. No matter what terrible thing has happened to me, and yes, a lot of it I was a victim. I know it wasn't my Daddy (Abbas) fault. In fact, I know it breaks His heart to see us in pain. It's our job to use all the evil for good to help others every day! This is what will and does bring the greatest joy more than you can imagine. All my pain was worth it if this helps someone!

God's timing isn't always our timing. When I got this job at Farb, God had me wait until my son was healed from all of his different problems and all the surgeries were paid for through Medi-Cal. God was so faithful. He was always taking care of us like a good Dad.

I'll never forget how nervous I was that first day of teaching at my new middle school. I was a PE teacher and I had the locker room all to myself and I decorated that stinky place for hours so that the girls would be so excited when they came in.

My office became a hub for all the students to come in and tell me all the problems that they had and everything that was going on so that I could advise them. Suddenly, I was starting to feel like a child myself which was wonderful. One of my favorite memories was the square dancing lessons. I did an entire month for this unit. I picked eighth graders that were somewhat successful in class but many of them were struggling with identity. I chose them to come to my locker room at lunch so that they could decide what couples would be great for square dancing. I was in awe of these children's discernment and wisdom. If we could all just see through the eyes of a child our hearts would be so open to so much more. Those amazing students took into account every emotion each student would have based on the dance partner that was chosen for them.

They picked partners for each student based on what would help them grow the most as a person, not just silly crushes they thought they might have. I would wipe away tears when they would leave my office. Their hearts were so good and so pure. I'll never forget the day I announced to each class their dance partner. Some shy kids were put with the popular kids that would be kind to them. I saw kids truly blossom into such generous loving humans during that month. That was an experience I still treasure. Those eighth graders are now in college and I pray they know what a difference they made for so many kids.

Everyone laughed at me because I made some pretty hilarious workout videos that my daughter filmed for me at the park and that was our every Friday. It was Boot Camp with Polly. Thursdays were the cougar run and I loved my partner that I worked with as he was the boys' coach and we were like brother and sister.

God always brought a support system around me even in my times of trouble. If you look at your own life you will see some kind of gift that is supporting you too.

Every single Thursday these kids would line up behind the tall fence until I blew the whistle. I would play super loud music and every lap I would mark for them and cheer them on. They had to run a certain amount of laps around the dirt field in order to get there A for the day. Truly some kids surprised me, even the chubby ones as they were out running the skinny ones because they weren't lazy. Now that I think about it, they also probably were trying super hard because they wanted the otter pops that I was going to give to them if they excelled. No matter what it was, I always felt blessed being around all these kids. Those days further solidified my relationship with who I was and who I was created to be.

On the weekends Carmen would have regattas all over the state. My mom would watch Wesley some of those weekends so that I could get up at three in the morning and drive her up there so that she could compete. One of the really fond memories I have is that I got to go to the regional finals. I guess they always called me the fun mom because I was the crazy one crazy enough to try to act their age! This particular time I thought that I would get on their torture device called the erg machine. I was going to show them how this lady could get it done and I started competing with one of the boy rowers who was on the machine right next to me. When I got back to camp they asked me why my face was almost purple and why were my pants wet. I realized at that point I Peed my pants when I walked back to the camp because I was in so much pain.

Getting old just sucks, can I get an amen? I had slipped a disc in my back and I ended up in the hospital when I got home. That was the longest 6-hour bus trip home ever. I couldn't even sit down. Both my children had to load me in the car and my daughter drove me to the hospital and put me in a wheelchair just so they could do an x-ray of my back. I was so grateful for my kid's man! I believe I learned my lesson in trying to prove myself to 16-year-olds, LOL Things on the home front were plugging along.

Wes was still working at the church and my kid's dad was still not really around. Carmen and I would go down to Mexico on mission trips when she wasn't rowing or it was her off season. These few times were some of the highlights of my life.

On one particular trip we drove down early in the morning and the object was to build a house in a day for a family. Now this family in particular were living in a cardboard box, the mom, the dad, 4 kids, and grandma and grandpa. This is only 30 minutes from my door. The poverty so close to home really breaks my heart.

We are the light in the world and we are to bring light to the dark places. In one day our team built four walls poured a foundation and made a little small outhouse these people are so thankful. When I think back to Grand mom's face she had the look of complete peace and thankfulness. If we all had such contentment with so little. My daughter and I both realized all the problems that we thought we had were nothing compared to the rest of the world.

I would just repeat the verse first Peter 57:10 that says, "cast all your cares upon Him for he cares for you. Be vigilant because your enemy the devil walks about like a roaring lion seeking whom he may devour. Resist him in faith knowing that the same sufferings are experienced by your brothers and sisters in the world."

Just like Job was protected but he lost everything and he still worshipped God and then in the end he got double for his trouble.

See I could look back and see all the times that I could have just been happy for what I had right in front of me. Now I'm an old lady and I see it all so clear. The devil or our mind steals our joy when we are in the middle of a crisis.

Those people in Mexico were living in a box with no bathroom and they still found joy. When we would go on these trips I would say, "God renew my faith and help me to be more like Job to be thankful in all things and cast all my silly cares on my Heavenly Father because you have never ever forgotten me. When I look back and think about that experience I realize God was always with my daughter and I and my son and this started developing a deep knowing inside my soul that my Heavenly Father had always been there.

I needed to let go of feeling like why wasn't I enough for my own dad.

RIGHT NOW PUT THIS BOOK DOWN AND LOOK AT ALL YOUR BLESSINGS EVEN IF IT'S JUST THIS BOOK. GRATITUDE CREATES A NEW ATTITUDE! YOU ARE LOVED DEEPLY. KNOW THAT!

"Train up a child in the way they should go and when they are old they will not depart from it." Taking my kids on mission trips, Carmen being faithful with Rowing, my son always showing up every Sunday at 4 AM and working until 9 o'clock at night, I know I knew then, no matter what, that my kids would be great.

Now that I was teaching school I could sell houses here and there in order to get ahead. When Carmen was in the 11th grade my son got an email saying that I had a sister. Now I already had a half-sister that I was super close to and another 1/2 sister that I was not close to, a half-brother that was in my life but not really a part of my life but I still really loved.

The internet wasn't around when I was a kid and my Mom didn't really want to communicate with all my Dad's exes for me to have a relationship with them and neither did their Moms. Through ancestry DNA I found another sibling that was adopted at birth. That relationship in the beginning was good, but after a while was quite a disappointment. However, that also led to the blessing of finding more siblings which I will tell you in the next book of God's redemption.

Here's the thing. If Wesley would had never been sick and on that computer all the time he would not have done ancestry DNA, which my mom bought for him so that he could fill some of his time. Then I probably never would've found her which means I probably would've never found my two other siblings that I just love so much.

The path to wholeness doesn't always look like what we think we just need to be able to ride the wave and know that God has our back. Now it's my second year teaching and I was going to be able to be full-time. I also was going to be teaching a college readiness class which I was super scared about but that was the only way I could be full-time. I decided, instead of being sad I would create a club called hope. My Hope Bible club in the beginning had 20 kids and at the end I had 250 children. Many received the Lord.

I'll never forget the sweet girl that I felt was being violated at home, she was touched by the Holy Spirit in class. I knew because when we were praying in class I said something simple like God protect all these precious kids when they walk in the door at home. At that moment she started violently weeping. That day and when we had our run, tons of kids ran up to me and said that she was hurting herself running. I saw her and there was blood pouring out of her arm. She had been cutting herself because her memories were starting to come to the forefront.

God wants us whole and totally healed. He doesn't want you to just have half of healing whether it's physically or mentally he wants an overhaul. He wants you to arise and walk into your destiny. Even though sometimes that may seem really painful to face the awful things that you've gone through, this little girl was manifesting what she felt on the inside.

I'll never forget every kid gathering around this young girl holding hands at a public school in San Diego praying that she would be delivered and released from her pain.

These are military kids and kids from all kinds of socio economic backgrounds between 12-14 years old. As they were praying her whole face changed and she just collapsed in my arms and told me everything that day. She sobbed on my shoulder and I had to call child protective services and she went directly into somewhere where she would be cared for and taken care of.

Right as she released the truth on that football field a countenance fell over her that looked like an angel and the wind blew onto the football field. That moment all the kids felt it at the same time, as if the spirit lifted off of her. I saw with my spiritual eyes 25-foot-tall angels flying to the field surrounding the entire field with their angel arms locked so that no other spirits could get to these children.

One of the kids asked do you see those angels that are surrounding the field, without me saying anything. I know without a doubt that the manifest presence of the Lord protecting His children was there.

If all that struggle I went through was for that little girl's freedom it was all worth it. Today she is back with her family. That person is in jail and she is thriving in college!

Satan wants to pervert the plans of God and he tries to do his work through people looking to see what you are giving place to. There are three things the devil tries to stop you from walking into you to your destiny, he will deceive you, he will accuse you, and he will persecute you.

The #1 thing that will always overcome Satan's sick plans is by knowing who you are that you are daughter or son of the creator of the world. That's what I told those kids that day and they knew it.

Wesley was just about to go into ninth grade my daughter was rowing her brains out. She got picked to be on the junior Olympic team and she was starting to really crush it and her grades were excel- ling, rowing was getting faster and faster and colleges from all over the country were giving her full ride scholarships.

See, my daughter never talked to her school about what had really happened to her. I am still in awe how both kids never played the poor me card ever! They could have said and used that we were all sharing one room, that their dad was in and out of rehab, everything that they had witnessed. They never accepted being a victim ever which I can't even believe how strong those 2 angels are. They never let the bad things that had happened to him dictate their future.

I have always told them when life gets tough God is working be- hind the scenes getting everything ready so that you can walk into what He has for you. See, we are all just in constant preparation of what's next.

When it was time to go on College Road trips, my mom was down for everything. We were going to Stanford, which was Carmen's dream school so that she could row for the week and my son and I got to be in San Francisco. I had lost my GPS and I was so worried about it and our group prayed. I was literally in a parking lot at Fry's warehouse going to buy a new one and God said, "trust me you're going to find it tonight." Before we left for our trip I looked in my shoe in the closet and there it was. We just have to trust and believe!

This is a picture that my daughter would always draw in church. She trusted God even though sometimes it was prickly. I'll never forget that awesome trip when we got to go up north and Wes and I got to play in the city when Carmen was at school. If I would have had to buy a new GPS I would not have been able to do anything fun with my son. After that trip we came home and I knew something was about to shift.

Carmen was starting to have tremendous pain in her hip when she would row and when I took her to the doctor at almost the end of her junior year she had a labral tear. This meant that she wouldn't be able to row for an entire year. I thought this can't be, which meant her scholarship to Harvard, Brown, possibly Stanford her dream school and all these schools she worked so tirelessly for might drop her including her dream school of Stanford.

When God takes you to something He takes you through something. Oh my sweet little girl her whole life would write me cards to make me feel OK with our situation and she was brokenhearted. Even right before that she had given me the sweetest little card I still keep in my purse.

When I was writing this book I was going through all the things that we went through in order to get her prepared for scholarships. I never had to worry about her life. It was filled with getting up early in the morning, getting ready for school doing papers, going to school get- ting everything prepared for college, coming home having a protein shake, going to practice till six, coming home doing homework till nine, her weekends were regattas and going to nutrition counselor's tu- tors, coaches for rowing. This was literally her entire life, and mine too. I was even reading one of the Bragg sheets that we did for her when she was getting her resume together to go to college to get scholarships. One of the questions was to note any achievements or insights regarding your student's leadership or her abilities?

This is what her school said about her at her rowing club:

"She was stated a stroke which means she is the leader of the boat. It is a position that is only given to responsible and trustworthy athletes. Carmen was immediately a stroke because the coach knew she would be able to lead and follow through. She has a brother that had many health problems growing up and she had to be self-motivated many times because her mother could not be there for her all the time, so she had to learn how to do it herself."

When I read her personal statement of everything she had been through, losing our home, losing her friends, living in one room, pretty much losing her dad, losing the income coming in so we could stay where we were, she never ever lost hope. I knew this was going to crush her. I read back over a prophetic word I got for her growing up. A prophetic word is like encouragement from another person that comes straight from heaven about the future. This is so important, if you have dreams or people that have spoken to you about your life you need to create a journal and start writing it down so that in times of trouble you can go back and read it.

In 2011, I wrote in a journal which was 4 years before this happened by the way, "Carmen will know what she's supposed to do, I will guide her like I did Abraham." I was worried about my son too, and it said "do not be afraid, I'm with your family I am their shield and I am there an exceedingly great reward." I read that over and over and over again trying to wrap my head around why this would happen to my kid. Through everything that has been happening over the years I was learning to hear that small quiet voice that would guide me and would show me the path I was on was correct.

Carmen knew that she couldn't row anymore she also knew that maybe she could start enjoying her life and not focus so much on per- forming but just being and learning to just let go and be happy.

That summer we got to enjoy just being a family and her not having to train for anything and just enjoying our self-knowing that the next year I'd be teaching again.

The following February, in her senior year, I decided to date one more time and met this professional hockey player guy. He was wonderful and on one of our dates he took me to the desert with motorcycles and had a bottle of wine and a tablecloth and he took me riding. He set a white linen tablecloth for dinner. I couldn't have asked for a nicer guy, he loved my kids, he was such a good person but he just wasn't for me. I went away on a three-day weekend that was a weekend to heal more from my past and forgive my father even more and when I came out of that weekend I called this young man and told him he just wasn't for me.

Now God 's timing is always the right timing and He renews your strength. God wants to renew your strength and He wants to exchange your strength for His. He is the deliverer and the refresher of our souls.

As I was getting prepared to write this book I was going through my prophetic journal and I found a dream that I had on December 26th, of 2010. I had a dream that all of my exes had found wives and then I was complaining to God why I could not find a husband and these are the words that I wrote that I heard God say in my dream. "Your steps even when you weren't following me when you got together with the neighbor I still was protecting you and leading you. The choices you have made have broken a generational curse on your family on your children's children and they will serve Me and your steps will be directed and your future husband is in the future."

Now at this point, Theodore was in a place called U-turn for Christ and he was finally starting to get sober and his new baby's mama was sober and had custody of the son. He was starting slowly but surely to get sober and realize that that life that he was living wasn't working and he moved into a nice place near his other son. He was still not really around the kids so it was really up to me to be there for them for every- thing but at least it wasn't how it was before.

Now after I forgave myself for not liking this new guy I got a phone call that March from a guy that I knew when I was 18 years old if you recall his name was Ryan. We never ever dated but he had called and I was starting to feel that feeling of, Wow God is this it? To be continued! God is good and He is there in the waiting!

Chapter 16

AN INTIMATE MESSAGE FROM GOD TO YOU - YOUR DADDY LOVES YOU

This was written by my dear friend and I believe that this is a message for every single person that's reading this book to know your

real identity. It is not that your dad didn't love you, or that he left you, or that your mom wasn't there for you, that you weren't good enough, or what was wrong with you none of that is true. I want you to read a letter **from God to you!**

"You may not know me, but I know everything about you." Psalms 139:1.

"I know when you sit down and when you rise up" Psalms 139:2. "I know all your ways and I still love you." Psalms 139:3.

"Even the very hairs on your head are numbered by Me and I know the number" Matthew 10:29-31.

"For you were made in My image." Genesis 1:27.

"In me you live and move and have your being." Acts 17:28.

"For you are my offspring I knew you even before you were conceived." Jeremiah 1:4-5.

"I chose you when I planned creation." Ephesians 1:11- 12.

"You were not a mistake. Did you hear that? You are not a mis- take for every single day you're alive is written in my book." Psalms 139:15 -16.

"I determined the exact time of your birth and where you would live." Acts 17:26.

"You are fearfully and wonderfully made." Psalm 139:14.

"I knit you together in your mother's womb." Psalms 139:13.

"And brought you forth on the day that you would be born." Psalm 71:6.

"I have been misrepresented by those who don't truly know Me." John 8:41-44.

"I am not distant and angry, but I am the complete expression of love," I John 4:16.

"And it is my desire to lavish my love on you." 1 John 3:1.

"Simply because you're my child and I am your Father." 1 John3:1.

"I offer you more than your earthly father ever could." Matthew 7:11.

"For I am the perfect Father." Matthew 5:48.

"Every good gift that you receive comes from My hand." James 1:17.

"For I am your provider and I meet all your needs." Matthew 6:31-33.

"My plan for your future has always been filled with hope." Jeremiah 29:11.

"Because I love you with an everlasting love." Jeremiah 31:3.

"My thoughts toward your account is the sand on the séashore." Psalm 139:17-18.

"I rejoice over you with singing." Zephaniah 3:17.

"I will never stop doing good to you." Jeremiah 32:40.

"For you are my treasured possession." Exodus: 19:5.

"I desire to establish with all my heart and all my soul." Jeremiah 32:41.

"And I want to show you great and marvelous   things." Jeremiah 33:3.

"If you seek me with all of your heart you will find me." Deuteronomy 4:29.

"Delight in me and I will give you the desires of your heart." Psalm 37:4.

"For it is I who gave you those desires." Philippians 2:13.

"I am able to do more than you could ever possibly imagine." Ephesians 3:20.

"For I am your greatest encourager." 2 Thessalonians 2:16-17.

"I am also the Father who comforts you and all your troubles." 2 Corinthians 1:3-4.

"When you're broken hearted I am close to you." Psalm 34:18.

"As a shepherd carries a lamb, I have carried you close to my heart." Isaiah 40:11.

"One day I'll wipe away every tear from your eyes." Revelation 21:3-4.

"I'll take away all the pain you've suffered on this earth because it was never my intention." Revelation 21:3-4.

"I am your Father and I love you even as I loved my son Jesus." John 17:23.

"For in Jesus, my love for you is revealed." John 17 :26.

"He is the exact representation of My being." Hebrews 1:3.

"He came to demonstrate that I am for you not against you." Romans 8:31.

"And to tell you that I am not counting your sins." 2 Corinthians 5:18-19.

"Jesus died so that you and I can be reconciled." 2 Corinthians 5:18-19.

"His death was the ultimate expression of my love for you." 1 John 4:10.

"See he was my only son and I gave up everything I love that I might gain your love." Romans 8:31-32.

"If you receive the gift of my son Jesus then you receive me." 1 John 2:23.

"And nothing you ever do will ever separate you from how much I love you." Romans 8:38-39;

"Come home and I'll throw the biggest party Heaven has ever seen." Luke 15:7.

"I have always been your Father and will always be your Daddy." Ephesians 3:14-15.

"My question to you my dear beloved is will you be my child?" John 1:12-13.

"I have been waiting for you." Luke 15:11-32.

Love,

Your Dad, Papa, Almighty God, Abba, Daddy

ABOUT THE AUTHOR
POLLY WALSHIN

I am a Southern girl at heart, living in San Diego for over 20 years. I have two amazing children now, ages 24 and 21. I live right around the corner from my mom, who has been my rock my entire life. I am now happily married to a wonderful man.

I wrote this book knowing it was time for me to reinvent myself as a mom and inspire others who could use my mess in my own life and help others not make the same mistakes.

I graduated from The American College with a degree in Interior Design in Atlanta, Georgia. I spent the first couple of years out of college working for a large Model Home company, designing over 100 homes for many builders.

My family and I were growing and decided to move to San Diego. I spent the next ten years as a homemaker and put my career on hold to be with my children.

When I became a single mother, my oldest was seven, and my youngest was five. When I got my real estate license, the market crashed in 2006, and my real estate career took off. I sold over $10 million worth of real estate in two years by knocking door-to-door and helping people get out of their homes without foreclosure. I was, at the time, the leader of the singles at my church.

I also helped open many LA Fitness Centers all over San Diego. I was their number one producer while still managing to be able to be there for my children for everything as a single mother.

In 2010 I went to work for Dunbar Armored and was the West Coast account executive of sales. I was the top producer on the West Coast for a couple of years, but this was not my calling.

I was so blessed at the same time to be a territory leader for the wonderful organization Moms In Touch. They help organize Moms at schools get together and pray for their kids and the kids at the schools. I wanted to help children know that nutrition and health are vital to their success.

While working a full-time job, being a single parent, and being a Girl Scout mom, Boy Scout mom, rowing sponsor for my daughter's team, and my son's soccer coach, I set out to return to school. At night I would write papers to get my Master's Degree in Education. I received my Master's in Secondary

Education and became a PE teacher in 2013. I taught PE and health until I was injured in 2017.

During my time as a teacher, I started a Bible club called Hope, and every week; we HAD OVER 200 STUDENTS. Before I left the school, we had over 200 salvations in a public school. I went back to selling real estate because I knew I could be successful, but this still needed to be fulfilled, and I could not teach anymore. I knew the best thing I could do was help others. I honestly had to reinvent myself again in my late 40s.

When the whole world was shut down during quarantine, I knew it was time to write my book. All of this overachieving goes back to a lack of not knowing the love of my father. So during quarantine, I wrote this book called Daddy Issues. This was the course that I was always supposed to be on. I also called out to the Lord, and He answered.

In 2021 I bought a business called I Sweat Lodge. This culminates everything that I am part of in my heart. It helps people know their bodies can heal by building their immune systems. It is an infrared wrap therapy business in La Jolla, California. I just had to get more life under my belt to help more people. Unfortunately, I HAD TO CLOSE MY DOORS IN 2022. Life is a roller coaster, and you can get through anything with Jesus by your side.

Remember, our mess can become our message!!

Polly Walshin

Your Body is Your Temple!!

CONTACT PAGE

Polly Walshin

Email Address:

infor@yougotdaddyissues.com

Website Address:

yougotdaddyissues.com